THE EXTRAORDI

D1149647

CONTENTS

APPENDICES

The Extraordinary Reader
Introducing INSEAK®, the simplest,
fastest and most effective speed-reading
strategy ever devised
2007 Edition
Clive Lewis & Anthony Landale

ISBN: 978-1-906070-03-8

Published by **Vale House Press**
Vale House
100 Vale Road
Windsor
Berkshire
SL4 5JL
Telephone +44 (0) 1753 866633
Website: **www.illumine.co.uk**

British Library Cataloguing in Publication Data
A catalogue for this book is kept in the public library

Typeset and designed by Rani Rai-Quantrill,
Printed and bound in the UK by DPS

INTRODUCTION

Most books on speed-reading are too long, too dull and too difficult to learn from ...

... this is the conclusion that most of the people on my training courses have come to about speed-reading books, and it is feedback that has certainly shaped my writing here. So what you have now started to read is a book that is concise, easy to grasp and, most of all, of real value. I hope that along the way you will also find it to be challenging, engaging and even inspiring.

It is also critical to emphasise, right up front, that this book does not simply set out to help you accelerate your reading pace. Yes, speed-reading is one of the skills I will cover, but what is especially exciting about The Extraordinary Reader is that it provides you with a simple, new and effective reading strategy. What this means is that it will teach you to assess which books and documents you want to read in detail, which you want to read at speed and which books you don't want, or don't need, to read at all.

However, in order to reap the full rewards of this new approach to reading you will have to be a willing learner, and that means you will need an open mind and will need to be prepared to practise. In this respect we are partners in this enterprise and, although I will do all I can to encourage you, it is inevitably up to you how much you get from the insights, exercises and reading strategies which I will go on to describe.

Let me say a little more about what this entails.

The problem that many people find when they set out to develop the skills of speed-reading, is that they are sceptical about the results they can achieve. They anticipate that when they read faster they will start to lose comprehension. They expect to find it hard to keep going and they start to wonder whether the claims made for speed-reading really add up.

You might ask why people tend to start out with such a negative perspective and the answer is that scepticism is a great way to protect ourselves from disappointment or from looking naive. It is also a sure way of proving to ourselves that our current behaviour is justifiable. But being sceptical is a killer for learning, so my request to you now is that you suspend your disbelief. By all means evaluate any claims made, and don't ignore what you know to be true, but if you are interested in harnessing your mind and building your speed-reading capability then bring a clear intent and a positive commitment to this project.

So having encouraged you to maintain a positive mindset, let me now just tell you a little more about what is possible with this approach, because it is important that you really want these following outcomes:

▶ this approach to reading will enable you to get through *all* the unread books, reports, magazines and emails that pile up in your office. *It will help you to eliminate information overload.*

▶ this book leads you through a range of speed-reading techniques which will enable you to assess, assimilate and absorb new knowledge and information easily and quickly.

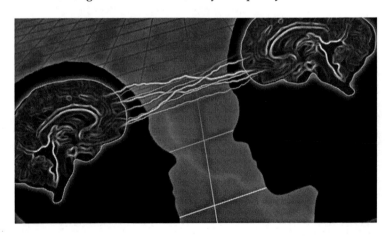

▶ you will be able to *triple your reading speed* (at least) and, at the same time, be able to enjoy reading just as much, if not more, than ever before.

▶ I will explain how you can understand more of what you read because of the effective ways in which you are using your brain.

▶ you will end up *remembering more* of what you read because of the powerful reviewing strategies you will learn in this book.

So are any of these claims surprising? They might be. But I have trained thousands of people in this approach and it works. It can work for you too and, when you have mastered this skill, you will find that it transforms your effectiveness at work.

START WITH THE END IN MIND

All the people I teach are entranced by the prospect of being able to read faster, understand better and remember more. They know that if they can achieve this it will make a remarkable difference to their lives. However, most of them are not sure of their own capabilities and when I then ask them 'how much faster do you want to be able to read?' I find that people's initial ambitions are fairly modest. Indeed, the people I teach are often reluctant to state any desired improvement in numerical terms.

This is not at all surprising because what people *really* want is to be able to read more effectively. And this typically includes:

▶ being able to understand the gist of what they are reading

▶ having a way to determine its relevance

▶ feeling confident that they will remember what they have read

▶ being able to link new information to what they already know

▶ being able to answer questions on what they have read e.g. for exams or presentations

▶ being able to relay new information and knowledge to others.

What people do not say is 'I want to be able to understand every word on every page' or 'I want to read faster than anyone else I know'. On the contrary, what people are indicating is that they want an improved reading performance which will allow them to acquire new information and knowledge with ease. Speed-reading is one of the ways in which people can get through the documents they receive but it is not, on its own, the whole solution.

INSEAK® - A NEW APPROACH TO READING

It is because reading effectiveness is such a priority that I have developed the INSEAK approach. INSEAK stands for **Intelligent Strategy for the Effective Acquisition of Knowledge** and is a comprehensive way for anyone who is faced with regular and large quantities of information to manage their workload. It incorporates the important aspects of objective setting, active reviewing, note-taking, flexing, skimming and scanning – and sets the skills of reading faster in the overall context of knowledge gain.

INSEAK can be applied to virtually any reading material including books, reports, proposals, memos, magazines and emails. It is entirely flexible in that readers are continually assessing as they are reading so they can choose to enter or exit the process at many different points. But what makes it so powerful is that it gives readers a framework, a way to direct their reading as well as to achieve total control. For all those people who are struggling to stay abreast of the constant arrival of new information INSEAK provides a practical solution to a very pressing problem.

THE START OF THE PROCESS

The content of this book is exciting and easy to understand. However, as with any new learning it may require a change in belief and behaviour from you so, in this respect, it might be challenging.

We read in the way we do for very good reasons. These include the way we have been taught, the enjoyment we get from reading, the sort of reading we do, the attitude we bring to reading and the relevance of reading to the work we do. And because we have been reading in our own particular way for many years, it can take time and effort to install a new skill or discipline.

I will talk about how to change habits and beliefs, and about how to manage your learning state later on in this book, but for now let us move on and begin the process of turning you into an extraordinary reader.

THE FOUNDATIONS

In this chapter I am going to outline some of the key research findings that underpin speed-reading. Let me emphasise immediately how important it is for you to recognise that there is a sound theoretical base to this approach. When you are learning a new skill it is vital that you are aligned in thought and deed. If, in your mind, you are not sure of the validity of an approach then guess what … at the first obstacle you will start listening to your doubts and may give up. Conversely, when you understand how and why a method operates then that provides the foundation for your swift and certain progress.

BRAIN POWER

"What seems astonishing is that a mere three-pound object, made of the same atoms that constitute everything else under the sun, is capable of directing virtually everything that humans have done: flying to the moon and hitting seventy home runs, writing Hamlet and building the Taj Mahal - even unlocking the secrets of the brain itself."

Joel Havemann, A Life Shaken

The above observation by Joel Havemann recognises the extraordinary capacity and potential of the brain. But what exactly do we know about this 'object' that is relevant for speed-reading?

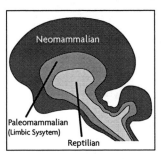

The research tells us that there are three distinctive parts to what has been termed the 'triune' brain. These are the base of the brain, called the reptilian brain, where the necessary command centres for living are located; the paleomammalian brain (including the limbic system), which promotes survival and refines and

SOME ASTOUNDING BRAIN FACTS

In his book *Mozart's Brain and the Fighter Pilot* Richard Restak highlights some astounding facts about the brain. He says that this 3lb object contains about 100 billion nerve cells or neurons along with an even greater number of non-neuronal cells called glia which are interspersed among the neurons. And it is these neurons that are responsible for the communication of information throughout the brain. Furthermore, Restak asks us to consider that the brain's outer wrinkled mantle, the cerebral cortex, contains about 30 billion neurons linked to one another by means of a million billion neuronal connections called synapses.

These are huge numbers but Restak goes on to point out that it would take more than 32 million years to count all of the synapses in the human brain at a counting rate of one synapse per second. And he suggests that if you concentrate on the number of possible neuronal connections (circuits) within the brain, you get an even more astonishing number: 10 followed by a million zeros. To put that number into some kind of perspective, Restak asks his readers to consider that the number of particles in the known universe comes to only 10 followed by seventy-nine zeros. And more than this, he says that the glia, which exceed the number of neurons by at least a power of 10, are also believed to be capable of communication. If this is true, then the number of possible brain states exceeds our most extravagant imaginings.

According to Restak any of the brain's 100 billion neurons can potentially communicate with any other via one or more linkages. Indeed, each neuron, he says, is no more than 2 or 3 degrees of separation from another. And linkages, once formed, are strengthened by repetition. At the behavioural level, this takes the form of habit. Each time you practise a piano piece or a golf swing (presuming you are doing it correctly), your performance improves. This corresponds at the neuronal level to the establishment and facilitation of neuronal circuits.

co-ordinates movement, and the neomammalian brain or cortex, which is responsible for the fine tuning of our lower functions and also for our associations, abstract thinking and planning capabilities.

However, in relation to speed-reading, perhaps the most important insight is our understanding that the brain divides into left and right hemispheres - and that these two hemispheres process information very differently. So, while the left-hand hemisphere of the brain is busy with words and numbers, order and logic, the right-hand hemisphere is constantly alert to the possibilities of shape and colour, rhythm and flow.

Another way of interpreting this is to consider that the left-brain provides us with our data and the right-brain provides us with a way of making data meaningful. And, of course, the really important finding is that everyone has a preferred, or dominant, side. If you have left-brain dominance it will mean that you have a preference for analysis and reason, structure and organisation. If you have right-brain dominance you will prefer holism and imagination, colour and spontaneity.

Of course, if you want to become a truly effective learner, it is your challenge to tap into the full capacities of both these hemispheres. Indeed, it is at this point that the words of one of the world's greatest creative talents, Leonardo da Vinci, come to mind:

"Study the art of science. Study the science of art.
Develop your senses, and do this in realisation that everything
connects to everything else"

Leonardo's suggestion that people should be looking to develop their potential also leads us to another hugely important finding from brain research - and that concerns the limbic brain. In essence, the research suggests that we have two brains: one, the rational brain, 'thinks' and the other, the limbic brain, 'feels'. And although in our everyday lives we 'think' of ourselves as rational beings, the truth is that the more intense our feelings become the more we lead with the limbic brain.

Does this have implications for learning? It certainly does. If you start on a speed-reading course because you 'think' it is a good idea but you are 'feeling' reluctant, anxious or even fearful of failure, then the chances of your success are just about zero. So, in addition to making logical choices about your decision to develop this skill you also have to address your feeling state (see more on learning states in chapter 7) and actively engage your limbic brain.

The way you need to go about this is to creatively engage with your purpose in wanting to learn this skill. How do you engage? Well, you can consider again why you are learning this approach (because it can triple your reading speed). And you can remind yourself how it will benefit you (by giving you more free time, more thinking time and less stress). And you can even check in with your beliefs e.g. 'I believe that this project could be enjoyable, stimulating and worthwhile'.

THE LIMBIC BRAIN AND HOW YOU LEARN

The limbic brain is 'the brain inside the brain'. Sometimes it is called the emotional brain because it is deeply tied into our feelings and our physical states.

Research shows that the limbic brain acts as the brain's emotion factory, creating the chemical messages that connect information into memory. This helps to explain how it is that in 'survival' situations we have the experience of acting before we think. This is the limbic brain at work.

In terms of learning this is relevant too. When we are emotionally engaged in learning we are setting our internal switch to 'high priority' and the impact of this is that it significantly improves our ability to retain information.

The real secret of success is
enthusiasm

In short, what you are doing here is resourcing yourself. Your limbic brain provides you with the key to your motivation. Without engaging your limbic brain you won't be successful, however hard you try. For all learning you need to stimulate your interest, your curiosity and your creativity – that is what will keep you going, and that is also what will make the learning stick. This isn't woolly thinking or being positive for the sake of being positive; it is brain science.

EYESIGHT, PERCEPTION AND BELIEF

Reading is all to do with your eyesight, isn't it? Well, yes. And then again, no. Just have a read of the panel opposite which will remind you what a newly developed skill reading is.

It is interesting to note John Ratey's view that we need both sound and sight to be effective readers. But when it comes to speed-reading there is another challenge that arises from our beliefs – whether we believe it is possible. For example, do you believe that:

- you can read more than one word at a time?
- you can expend less energy when you are reading faster?
- you can maintain comprehension when you are reading faster?
- you can recall more when you are reading faster?

All these questions may have you answering 'no' but they are all proven to be true. Your first challenge is to believe that they are truly possible for *you*.

You can find out more about the interface between eyesight and reading as you go through this book, but let me now just highlight the essential facts about the way we read and how this relates to the technique of speed-reading.

When asked, most people assume that they read in a smooth left to right motion across the page. However, our eye movements

VISUAL AND VERBAL APPROACHES TO READING

In his book *A User's Guide to the Brain*, John Ratey highlights the fact that while oral language has been around for tens of thousands of years the ability to represent sounds in written symbols i.e. through writing and reading has only been around for the last 5000. Moreover he says that it is only in the last century that reading and writing has become widespread - and from this he concludes that the neural mechanisms involved in reading and writing probably didn't evolve for these purposes. Rather, he suggests, that extensive teaching and practise through years of schooling are necessary for such mastery.

This is interesting background information for anyone who wants a better understanding of how the function of reading is organised in the brain. According to Ratey words that we see on the page are processed as single letters grouped together and this process is distinct from the visual perception we have of everything else. So we process words as visual units and recognise whole words as fast as single letters. Reading and our understanding of text is further speeded up by the regularity with which words are used and by our previous knowledge.

There is also ample evidence, says Ratey, that we visually process words along parallel routes of sight and sound, each with its own separate neural system. This makes perfect sense when you consider that there are people who read primarily by sight and those who read primarily by sound. Indeed, these two independent routes explain why some children learn to read better with phonics – sounding out words – while others learn better with whole language techniques where the whole visual word form is learned in context. Although most of us, says Ratey, use both pathways simultaneously and learn to read by combining the two systems.

The jumping movements when we read, called saccades, take approximately 20 milliseconds, while the pauses, called fixations, last approximately 150 to 300 milliseconds. It is only during the fixations, when the eyes are still, that reading occurs.

when we read are not smooth at all. Our eyes have to stop to take in information (fixations) and this means that instead of reading in a continuous flow we actually take a series of small jumps (saccades) as we read across the page.

The time you spend on fixations are a key determinant of your reading speed. If you take a long fixation, reading your document word by word, you will be a slow reader. Furthermore, if you skip back over words or re-read whole paragraphs, as most people do, then this will further handicap you.

The first question then is this. Is it possible to spend less time on each fixation and therefore learn to accelerate your reading speed? The second question to ask is whether it is possible to take in more words with each fixation. We will deal with these important questions and more in the following chapters.

YOUR PERSONAL LEARNING STYLE

As well as understanding the way in which your eyes take in information, it is also relevant to consider the way in which you process information – and in this respect some of the research coming out of NLP (Neuro Linguistic Programming) has been ground-breaking.

At the heart of NLP lies the understanding that although we share the same senses – sight, hearing, touch, taste and smell – we filter information about the world through these senses very differently. So, for example, some people filtering through their visual senses may *look* for the big picture, *see* what is possible or declare a point of *view*. Others will make sense of the world through their auditory sense; for example they may be interested in people who *speak* the same language as themselves, they may need to make themselves *heard* or might be interested in *tuning* into new ideas. And then there are people who filter information kinaesthetically; for example they may need to get their *teeth* into a project or get to *grips* with everything involved before they feel able and confident to proceed.

This finding has implications for people who want to improve their ability to manage information and acquire knowledge. Firstly, it points to the fact that you may find it harder to take in information that is written in a different preference to your own.

More than this, however, this research finding suggests that you will need a storage system for the information that you take in that is personal to you. That is why I emphasise Mind Mapping as such a critical aspect of the INSEAK approach. In essence, Mind Mapping is a key technique for you to learn because it helps you to encode the information you have just read. It allows you to do this quickly and effectively through the use of key words, symbols, colour and associative imagery in ways that appeal to the senses. Such stimulation triggers a kinaesthetic response and has been found to be tremendously valuable in supporting memory and recall.

I will talk in much more detail about Mind Mapping later but there is one more point to make here about reading preferences and learning styles.

Reading is, of course, a technique that combines visual and verbal preferences. Most of us learned to read by speaking, one letter, and then one word, at a time before being asked to read quietly, in our heads. As a result of this teaching strategy many people still sub-vocalise as they read. However, this is not the best tool for the job. 'Eye to mind' is much quicker than 'mouth to ear' and it is this advanced strategy of reading that I will be emphasising in this book.

> Research shows that some deaf people, with no special reading training, can read over 1000 words per minute, because they do not translate words into sounds.
> *Road to Reading Project*

Let me stress, however, that there is still a place in reading for those of you with advanced auditory skills. When we really want to make a piece of information stick, one of the best strategies is to vocalise it. And the use of music as an aid to learning is an integral part of what has become known as accelerated learning. So don't think that auditory or kinaesthetic preferences are somehow subservient to visual preferences – this would not be true.

What is apparent, however, is that our understanding of how we think and learn and communicate our preferences is relevant. In this respect I simply encourage you to get to know what preference you lead with and then to expand your range by practising other styles.

DEVELOPING LEARNING STYLE FLEXIBILITY

Another model of how we learn is that developed by Honey and Mumford called 'Learning Styles'. In this model people have learning preferences divided into the following four categories.

▶ *Activists* like to leap up and have a go, they learn by doing.

▶ *Reflectors* like to think about things before trying anything new. They learn by watching others.

▶ *Theorists* like to understand the theory and to have a clear grasp of the concept before applying a new skill.

▶ *Pragmatists* like to have some practical tips and techniques from someone with experience before trying something new.

This is directly relevant to reading. For example, if you are a theorist and are reading, say, a 'how to' book authored by a pragmatist you may find it hard to take in the information. As with NLP, the solution to this conundrum is to develop your 'flexibility' and stretch into those learning styles which may not be so comfortable for you but which are just as valid as your own.

MAKING AND BREAKING HABITS

"The beginning of a habit is like an invisible thread, but every time we repeat the act we strengthen the strand, add to it another filament, until it becomes a great cable and binds us irrevocably, thought and act."

Orison Swett Marden

The development of learning styles leads us directly onto the question of our everyday habits and patterns of behaviour. We may have developed a style of reading, for example, not because it is the easiest way to read but through poor teaching or careless practice. So some people even late in life still sub-vocalise when they read even though it is a slow reading strategy.

My contention here is that the habits you choose will determine your outcome. So when it comes to reading, how healthy are your habits? If you want to achieve the objectives you have set yourself, then you may need to challenge your long established patterns, be willing to try out new techniques and be motivated to practise.

However, this is not just a case of will-power. Neuroscience (the study of the brain) shows us that our habits create neural pathways – literally patterns in our brain that we form by habitual ways of thinking and behaving. If we deliberately choose a different behaviour, and continue to practise it, then over time we will create a new neural pathway. This new behaviour will, quite literally, become our preferred pattern and the old pathway will start to diminish.

That being said, you have to take positive action if you want to establish a new habit – and outlined over the page is a strategy which you can adopt to ensure that you are fully prepared in your intention to become an extraordinary reader.

STRATEGY FOR INSTALLING A NEW HABIT

1. What do you want? Be clear and state what you want in the positive. For example, 'I want to read at 800 words per minute' is far more likely to help you achieve your aim than 'I want to stop feeling stressed by all the documents I am sent'. That is like trying not to think of a pink elephant – you will get the result you don't want.

_____

_____

2. How will you know when you have achieved it? What is the evidence you will need? Think about what you will see, hear and feel when you have reached your desired outcome.

_____

_____

3. Ask yourself how you can start and maintain your move towards this outcome. Consider the attitude and support required.

_____

_____

4. Be clear about your timescale. How long is this going to take and by what date do you want to become an extraordinary reader?

_____

_____

5. Check to see if there is any benefit you are getting from your current reading strategy that you might wish to preserve e.g. there may be times when it is important for you to read slowly.

_____

_____

6. Check also that the energy, time and cost that you will be putting into speed-reading is worth it and is in keeping with your sense of who you are.

_____

_____

"Everything you see and touch was once
an invisible idea until someone chose
to bring it into being.
Any **powerful idea** is absolutely
fascinating and absolutely useless
until we choose to use it"
Richard Bach

HABITS AND NEUROSCIENCE

"Until one is committed there is hesitancy, the chance to draw back, always ineffectiveness. The moment that one definitely commits oneself then providence moves too" W. H. Murray

Neuroscience is the study of how the brain works and it relates directly to memory and behaviour.

In essence, before every action we take our brain searches for neuro-associations which are recorded in our nervous system and which we use as landmarks for an appropriate response. For example, every time we cross the road we check for traffic because we have a vast store of neural associations that remind us that, if we don't then we could be involved in an accident.

This is directly relevant to any efforts we make to develop new behaviour. When we begin a new task we don't have the necessary neural associations to guide us. To illustrate this, think of what happens when you move your waste-paper basket from one side of your desk to the other. For some days afterwards you will keep turning to the old place before the new behaviour is installed.

In order to install a new behaviour you need commitment, repetition of the action and emotional intensity. In this way, each time you behave in the desired new fashion you will be building up a new neural pathway until you have a major, automatic route through to that required behaviour.

And this, of course, is why so many people fail when they try to change. They 'think' that wanting it will be enough; but they don't build up the neural pathways they need through regular practise. As a result their hoped for change comes to nothing. In contrast the strategy outlined on page 20 provides the framework for powering up your commitment and establishing a sure way to achieve your desired outcomes.

MEMORY STRETCHING

When it comes to memory the objective to have in mind is that we want to 'read faster, understand better, remember more' – and for most people it is 'remembering more' that is the real prize. It is this aspect of learning that I want to address next.

First and foremost, I want to remind you of this key point – that interest in the skills you are developing and the content you are reading are essential to memory. In the pyramid below you will see that the foundation stone is interest. It is your engagement in what you are doing that ensures your interest is maintained and that new information becomes understood, learned and remembered.

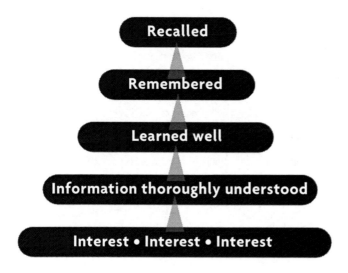

In addition to this, however, we know some pertinent facts about memory and our ability to recall information. First, we know that it easiest to recall information that we have read at the beginning and end of a study period. What we have read in the middle of a reading project, particularly if we have spent too long reading at a single stretch, is much harder to recall.

INFORMATION ON BREAKS

Take breaks every 25/45 minutes depending on ...
- the complexity of the material
- your interest level
- your physical needs
- your surroundings
- the quantity of work

What to do on breaks?
- move, dance, walk
- play music, talk
- take light refreshment
- get fresh air
- have fun, be creative
- relax, daydream

The way to improve your ability to recall information is easy to achieve. It is this. Create more breaks during those times when you are learning.

How long those breaks should be will depend on the difficulty of the reading material, your interest level, your attitude and alertness and your surroundings. However, the recommendation is to take a break every 25 – 45 minutes during such times of study.

It is also important to consider what to do during these breaks. I do not suggest the complete absence of activity. On the contrary, the best strategy is to engage in alternative actions that will help to revitalise you. So consider moving or walking, having a light refreshment, getting some fresh air, doing something that is enjoyable or fun, or taking a few minutes to practise conscious relaxation.

REVIEW STRATEGIES

To improve your ability to recall key information the most effective strategy is to review
- after one hour
- after one day
- after one week
- after one month
- after three months

The second strategy to adopt, if you want to recall more of what you have studied, is to ensure that you review what you have learned at regular intervals after your initial study time – see panel.

If you fail to review your work then 80% of the information that you have just taken time to read will be lost within one to two days and this is extremely inefficient. However, you can completely reverse this trend by making sure you regularly review what you have learned. And, of course, where you need to commit your learning to memory – e.g. for exams or presentations – applying yourself in this way can make all the difference.

MEMORY RHYTHMS DURING LEARNING

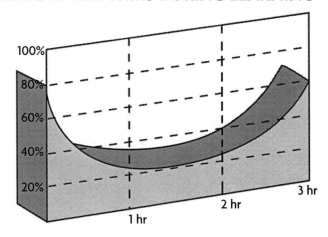

We remember most at the beginning and the end of every period of learning activity. If we can take breaks (every 45 minutes or so) during a sustained period of learning then we will boost our ability to recall information

Again Mind Mapping is a reviewing technique to be thoroughly recommended here because it will enable you to code the information you want to remember creatively and concisely – and will allow you to take in, at a glance, the key themes and ideas contained in what you have read. It is also much easier and quicker to go back to a Mind Map to review a subject than to go back to the original reading source to extract the key information all over again – see more on Mind Mapping on pages 41-45.

MIND MAP SKELETON. BUILD YOUR OWN LINKS
AND ASSOCIATIONS TO SUMMARISE THIS CHAPTER

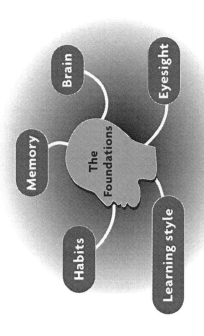

EFFECTIVE READING
INTRODUCING THE INSEAK® APPROACH

After teaching thousands of people how to speed-read I can honestly say that not one of them has ever claimed that they want to read faster in order to be able to boast that they can read at 800, 900 or over a 1000+ words per minute. So why are they attracted to this subject? What is their motivation? It is quite simple. They want to be able to read more effectively.

However, what it means to be able to read effectively will vary from person to person. It may include any, or all, of the following:

- being able to manage, and get through quickly, a continuous stream of reading material
- being able to understand and absorb information quickly
- being able to recall information easily
- having a flexible reading approach
- being able to enjoy reading.

So how can these objectives be met? The answer is in recognising that we need a powerful strategy that enables us to deal with all the written documents that we are faced with.

The Intelligent Strategy for the Effective Acquisition of Knowledge (INSEAK) is such a strategy – and it is based around the principle that we do not need to read everything that we are sent or given at work. On the contrary, one of the first freedoms that INSEAK allows us is the recognition that a great deal of the information that we receive, and which then piles up on our desks, shelves and email boxes, may not be relevant or appropriate for us to read at all. So how do we identify the nuggets we need? The answer to this is through the use of continuous assessment tools and techniques which can take us from preliminary understanding to the full assimilation of new knowledge.

INSEAK® - INTELLIGENT STRATEGY FOR THE EFFECTIVE ACQUISITION OF KNOWLEDGE

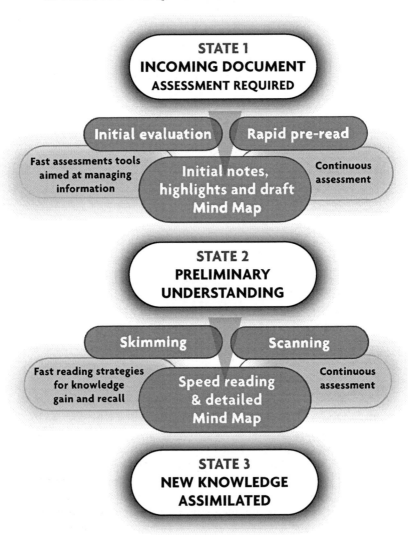

STATE 1
INCOMING DOCUMENT
ASSESSMENT REQUIRED

Initial evaluation

Rapid pre-read

Fast assessments tools aimed at managing information

Initial notes, highlights and draft Mind Map

Continuous assessment

STATE 2
PRELIMINARY
UNDERSTANDING

Skimming

Scanning

Fast reading strategies for knowledge gain and recall

Speed reading & detailed Mind Map

Continuous assessment

STATE 3
NEW KNOWLEDGE
ASSIMILATED

THE INSEAK® SYSTEM EXPLAINED

State 1: Incoming document – assessment required

Your reading strategy starts with the understanding that when a document arrives on your desk you are in a neutral state. In other words you do not know whether the documents, reports, books, magazines and emails that you have been sent require your attention or not. Your first and immediate objective then is to find out whether these documents need to be read, need to be delegated or can be ditched.

To help you make this assessment, INSEAK provides you with three fast and powerful tools – the initial evaluation, the rapid pre-read and the draft Mind Map. I will describe what these are, and how they work, in more detail in the next section of this chapter but suffice it to say for now that these tools are designed to help you establish, with the minimum of effort, what any document is about and whether you need to give it any further consideration.

State 2: Preliminary understanding

After you have conducted your initial assessment you arrive at the second state which INSEAK defines as 'preliminary understanding'. You now know which documents need your attention and, broadly, what they cover. However, you are still in assessment mode and, having gained your preliminary understanding, you now have to decide at what speed, and to what depth, you need to read those documents which you have determined are important.

You have another batch of techniques which you can use in this process– namely, skimming, scanning and speed-reading. You also need to include here how to use Mind Mapping as a powerful coding and reviewing tool.

The critical insight here is that your goal is 'sufficient knowledge'. For some documents this may be achieved by a skim read. In other cases you will choose to go through a series of reads each of which is more detailed. In this respect you are building up and

reinforcing your knowledge as you proceed and this process of multi-layering is a key characteristic of the INSEAK approach.

State 3: New knowledge assimilated

Just to re-emphasise the point, you will not need to apply every INSEAK tool to every document you read. Assessment is a continuous process and typically in business you will be mining for information rather than reading for pleasure. However, when you do require a thorough understanding of a document, INSEAK will lead you to the third state of 'new knowledge assimilated'.

Moreover, in addition to having gained the new knowledge you required, INSEAK will also have led you through a process of generating a robust reviewing strategy – your detailed Mind Map - which will have clarified and coded all the key information you need for easy recall.

There is more to come on how to Mind Map later but let me just say for now that, as well as being a powerful technique in its own right, the drafting of your Mind Map is also a signal that you have met your reading objectives and have completed the task in hand.

WHY ASSESSMENT IS SO IMPORTANT

In this chapter the focus is specifically on reading effectiveness. This is critical both for eliminating information overload and acquiring new knowledge with ease. You have to remember that while knowledge and information is the fuel for your career success, a core skill that executives need is to be able to filter for gold among all the gravel. Just consider for a moment ... when you pick up a document or magazine what are you looking to get out of it – factual information, learning, current news? You need clear objectives and a fast way to assess the value of such reading material.

Of course we are all always assessing when we read but, typically, this is an unconscious process. We filter for interest and relevance, for meaning and learning. But we can be much more effective when we make this a conscious approach.

To make a comparison, think of a casual male visitor at an art gallery. He wanders around the exhibition waiting for something to grab his attention. With such an attitude he is unlikely to find anything to be of more than passing interest because, quite simply, he doesn't know what he is looking for.

In contrast, take another male visitor who knows what he wants to find and who therefore enters the gallery with a much sharper focus. He looks for pictures painted by particular artists or covering a particular subject. If there are none to be found then he may, or may not, decide to spend more time there. But if he does find something in which he is interested then he will look at it in much more detail. He will go closer to those works of art which he is studying, looking at the perspective, the detail, the use of shade, the colour and the texture. And if he wants even more information then he might go as far as to buy a biography or listen to a tape which provides further insights or information about the artist in question.

The INSEAK system mirrors this process. It provides a focused approach to reading, helping you to find a fast way through to the key themes, concepts and ideas contained in any document, book or magazine. So let me now provide you with a more detailed explanation of the tools which are included in this approach.

TOWARDS PRELIMINARY UNDERSTANDING

Remember that when any document arrives in your in-tray, or in your in-box, your state is neutral. You do not know whether these missives require your attention or not. Quite naturally your task at this stage is to evaluate these documents. And you do not have to go into an in-depth study to make your decision.

Assessment tool 1: The initial evaluation

The initial evaluation is a primary tool in your assessment kit-bag. In a very short space of time it allows you to find out what the document in front of you is all about, what ground it is covering and what its promise is to you, the reader.

In order to make this a practical exercise I suggest that you find yourself a book or magazine – any title will do – from your shelves. Then follow these steps:

▶ Start by looking briefly at the front cover of the book or magazine. What does the title suggest? If there is a graphic or picture what does it convey?

▶ Now look at the back cover. Is there any useful information provided there? If it is a book see what the reviewers say and also check to see if there is a book flap which might provide a summary of the main themes or a reviewer's comment.

▶ Read the Table of Contents to understand the structure of the book or magazine. What do the chapter titles or headlines tell you?

▶ And finally read the introduction and the final paragraph - or if it is a magazine read the foreword by the Editor. This should give you a good idea of the scope of the material and where you are heading. Like the box in which a jigsaw puzzle comes, you are looking for the overall picture and a way to orientate yourself.

Of course this initial evaluation may need to change slightly if, for example, you are reading an article or a report. In the case of an article you would be looking at the title, the summary, the sub-headings and probably the first and last paragraphs. However, the thrust of your evaluation would be the same, namely, what ground is this piece of writing covering, is it interesting and/or relevant and, if it is not relevant, do you need to pass it on to someone else, or should you ditch it?

Assessment tool 2: The rapid pre-read
In every book, article and report there are only a few big ideas. The rapid pre-read helps you to identify what these are without wasting time on what you already know.

Let us say that your initial evaluation has helped you decide that the document you are reading is worth more of your time. Do you immediately start reading in detail? Absolutely not. You can use the next technique in the INSEAK approach which will help you to assess how much of it you need to read and to what depth.

The rapid pre-read is a powerful ten minute technique designed to help you extract and code the key information entailed. You are still assessing here - but in more detail. Here is the way to conduct it.

- Make a note of the time and allow yourself ten minutes (this would be ample for a 250–300 page book). Set an alarm if it helps. This deadline is your prompt to maintain your attention and momentum.

- Think clearly about your objectives. What do you want to get from the pre-read? Are you looking for general information, trends, comments, statistics? The clearer you are about your desired outcome the sharper your focus will be.

- Remind yourself about the ground that the book or magazine is covering. Do you have to look at it all? If not, just go to the sections that you are interested in.

- Now take your book or magazine and start turning the pages every one or two seconds. As you go along make a mental note of how the information is laid out. What are the trigger words that draw your eye? What passages, facts or comments interest you? Highlight those parts that you want to explore in more detail. Use bookmarks or post-its or thumb down the corners of the pages. But don't get stuck. Keep going.

- Do a quick review and complete a draft Mind Map of what you have just previewed. As an example of this, see the Mind Map at the end of this chapter. Your objective is, similarly, to produce a visual map which outlines and distinguishes the key themes of the material you have just read.

You should not have to spend more than ten minutes on the draft Mind Map. Simply revisit the contents and your notations to remind yourself of the key themes and issues. Then write down the topic of the book or magazine and draw onto your map lines that radiate out from that central word. Above each line write a word that represents a key theme. Remember, at this stage, you should not get drawn into the detail – your map only represents the big picture and will, inevitably, be incomplete.

As you would expect I am in the habit of Mind Mapping every business book that I read. I do not know, when I draw up my Mind Map, if I will ever want or need to read this particular book again – but I am confident that if I have that requirement I can go straight to my Mind Map which I always place in the back of the book. And what I will find there will not only be the big ideas presented clearly, but also associated ideas drawn from my own experience which I have included because they seemed to be relevant. One look at the Mind Map and all this information is available to me and I can recall almost everything I need.

The rapid pre-read is only a start, of course, but it may be all you need to do. Remember that with the INSEAK system you are reading for information and knowledge and are trying to assess every document for its relevance and value. Just read the case study overleaf to see how this approach works in practice.

Assessment tool 3: Highlighting and notetaking

In addition to completing a draft Mind Map, a key part of the INSEAK approach lies in getting used to highlighting and notetaking as part of the assessment process. These techniques are important and the advice I am now going to offer may shock some of you ... you must be prepared to write and make notes on the pages of your books, reports and documents.

Some people find this challenging because they feel that by making such notes they are devaluing the book or report they have just read and are also making it difficult for anyone else to read. This is

CASE STUDY: THE RAPID PRE-READ

I was recently working with John, a lawyer, who told me that he regularly receives large reports in the morning. These reports are up to 300 pages long and are full of detailed legal information. By the afternoon John has to be able to run client meetings based on these documents. So how can he possibly read and absorb so much data?

The solution John found was to use the rapid pre-reading technique on his reports, deliberately turning the pages so that he quickly gained an insight into the case or project at hand. But importantly, as he previewed these documents, he highlighted those sections which were critical or which he needed to read in more detail. This allowed him to bypass areas he knew and to spend more time on areas which he needed to understand better or particular issues of concern.

For a man in John's role, rapid pre-reading has proven to be essential. This is a practical solution for a workload that might otherwise be unmanageable.

a valid concern – but just compare for a moment the value of your time to the value of the documents that you typically have to read. Most of the reading material you will have to assess in business is disposable.

So why are highlighting and notetaking necessary? The reasons are as follows. When you are intent on highlighting key passages in the text, or writing notes in the margin, you are helping to prevent your mind and eye from wandering. More than this, these techniques engage you by asking you to recognise the key messages in what you are reading. And highlighting and note taking also help with the recall of data and information. I will talk more about recall later but if you want to retain information then reviewing your material is vital and what you are doing with highlighting and notetaking is giving yourself a fast way to get to the priority information.

HIGHLIGHTING AND NOTETAKING REMINDERS

✓ DO - use a marker pen, underline key words, circle important passages, jot margin notes, use post-its, dog-ear important pages.

✗ DO NOT - mark more than two or three items per page or write notes in too much detail.

BEYOND THE PRELIMINARIES

If you have followed the INSEAK approach you are already multi-layering – that is, coming at your document, book or magazine with different strategies and deepening your comprehension each time. Such big picture evaluation strategies only take minutes to complete but they provide a surprisingly good level of insight. Now you have to decide whether you want to read further and increase your depth of understanding. If you do then here are a range of fast reading strategies that can help you go beyond the preliminaries.

It is worthwhile noting that throughout this process you will be assessing continuously. At any time you can decide you have enough information and can bail out. A further skim or scan may be all you need. Each time you go through the material you will be picking up more data and you do not need to use every single technique on every document you read.

Reading strategy 1: Skimming

Skimming is a super fast reading technique which enables you to catch the headlines, identify specific areas of interest and/or get a sense of the story being told.

You need to skim when you have a great deal of information to get through and when you want to save time. But what are you

"What we see depends mainly
on what we look for"
Sir John Lubbock

doing when you skim read? In practice you are flicking through the document looking for those devices put into the text by authors as signposts to their readers. These include chapter headings, sub-headings, illustrations and captions, summaries and conclusions, pull out boxes or panels, case studies, quotes and bullet points.

Skimming is a more advanced strategy than the rapid pre-read which was primarily concerned with evaluation. You skim read to build on the information you picked up then. The rapid pre-read gave you the framework and now you are looking for additional data in those parts of the document that you have decided you need to know more about.

Skimming - self assessment exercise

Find the article 'Cutting the Bull' on page 97 and skim read it. Take no more than 30 seconds and then answer these questions

1. What were the main headlines? _____

2. What were the conclusions? _____

3. What else stood out for you? _____

4. Do you now have a preliminary understanding?   Yes/No

Reading strategy 2: Scanning

Scanning is another fast reading technique – but this one helps you to look for specific information. In the case of scanning you are not trying to understand overall meaning or sense – you are looking for detail or recognisable content. For example, you would scan when you are looking up phone numbers in a directory, or browsing schedules, catalogues or web pages for specific data. You would also use scanning when you want to find specific information in an article, document or book.

Hints on scanning:

▶ Get clear on exactly what you are looking for. Write down key words as this process will focus your mind on the key questions to which you want answers.

▶ Don't read every word. Let your eyes move to the key phrases, words or detail you are looking for – they will jump out at you.

▶ Use clues on the page such as chapter titles to guide you.

▶ Get into the author's head. How have they arranged their document? If it is an A–Z type document then only scan the section that you need.

Scanning – self assessment exercise

Take another look at the article 'Cutting the Bull'. See how fast you can find the following pieces of information

1. John Davies   2. Cluster technique   3. CO_2 emissions

How long did that take you?

☐ less than 30 seconds   ☐ less than 60 seconds
☐ about a minute   ☐ more than a minute

Reading strategy 3: Speed-reading

All the techniques I have mentioned so far fit into the INSEAK approach and so does speed-reading. However, when I use the term speed-reading I am referring to a particular set of techniques which will enable you to double or triple your current reading speed and which I will examine in more detail in the next chapter.

It should be noted at this stage, however, that there is an overlap between skimming, scanning and the advanced techniques of speed-reading. My advice here is not to get overly concerned about where one technique begins and another ends. When you are skimming and scanning you are not trying to read for in-depth comprehension. Similarly, when you are reading at the highest speeds possible there will be some content that you miss. Do not let this concern you. When you are using these high level, advanced speed-reading techniques you have a different purpose in mind – you are in big picture mode – and if you need more detail then you can return to those content-focused speed-reading techniques which allow you to achieve this objective.

So keep your mind on what you are trying to achieve as an outcome of this process – namely to manage all the information you receive, find effective ways to assess it and then to develop techniques that help you to read it fast. The INSEAK approach is a unique framework that will enable you to achieve all of this.

THE DETAILED MIND MAP

Mind Mapping is a technique that is quite distinct and extremely complementary to speed-reading. I recommend it because it helps people to capture, in a concise and memorable format, the information they have just read. For anyone interested in absorbing and recalling knowledge this makes it extremely valuable. I now want to go through in more detail how you can begin to Mind Map.

Flexibility is a key quality required in Mind Mapping and is one, once you have started practising, that you will find you are able to develop easily. The key is to start practising.

And remember – there is no single right way to Mind Map. It is your map so use your own ideas and creativity. In this book I have used specialist software to create my Mind Maps - but that isn't essential. Indeed it can be more creative to draw up Mind Maps by hand. Just to prove this point compare the Mind Maps on pages 43 and 45. The former is a map about Mind Mapping generated through software. The latter, which is all to do with planning a business trip, is hand generated. Both maps are equally valid and both use the techniques outlined in the following section.

KEY TECHNIQUES IN MIND MAPPING

The process of Mind Mapping may be simple but there are some key techniques contained within it which are well worth pointing out to the beginner.

1. How to start

Take a blank piece of A4 paper and turn it on its side. Start in the centre and draw an image and/or a word that represents the topic you are working on. This central image represents what your topic or issue is all about so making it stand out. Be bold. Ideally use colour and imagination.

2. Use

As you build your Mind Map you will be creating a structure characterised by lines, words and images radiating from your central image. I would encourage you to use a different colour for each of the main themes as it helps to separate out your ideas. Write single words written above the lines to define what each of these themes are about. One word per line helps clarity and comprehension and also enables better recall.

3. Lines

Vary the thickness of the lines radiating out from your central image. The thickness of the line denotes its relative importance. The main themes, often called the Basic Ordering Ideas (BOIs), are your key associations to the central issue so will be represented with the thickest lines. Ideas or associations branching off from these BOIs will then be represented by thinner lines.

4. Style

Mind Mapping is a personal process. There is no single 'right' way. You will have your own associations, your own graphic style and phrases and images that are meaningful to you. The guiding principle is to use image, colour, dimension and spacing in a way that appeals to you. That is what will make your Mind Map and the information coded within it powerful and memorable. Also

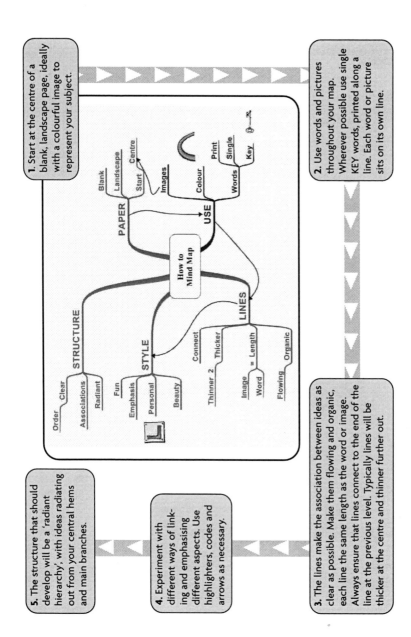

1. Start at the centre of a blank, landscape page, ideally with a colourful image to represent your subject.

2. Use words and pictures throughout your map. Wherever possible use single KEY words, printed along a line. Each word or picture sits on its own line.

5. The structure that should develop will be a 'radiant' hierarchy', with ideas radiating out from your central hems and main branches.

4. Experiment with different ways of linking and emphasising different aspects. Use highlighters, codes and arrows as necessary.

3. The lines make the association between ideas as clear as possible. Make them flowing and organic, each line the same length as the word or image. Always ensure that lines connect to the end of the line at the previous level. Typically lines will be thicker at the centre and thinner further out.

add your personal touch to your map. Include pictures, diagrams and symbols as this will further aid recall.

5. Structure

Mind Mapping is characterised by its radiant structure and once you have started practising drawing your own maps you will quickly become accustomed to the process. Mind Maps are a way of organising and presenting information in a visual way which correlates with the way our minds actually work. We don't think in lists or long essays - we think in images and key themes, shapes and patterns, all connected one to another. So start practising today.

Mind Mapping exercise

1. Take a book or magazine from your shelves and, on a blank piece of paper (landscape), draw an image that represents it.

2. Conduct a rapid pre-read of the book or magazine. See what ground it is covering, how it is structured and what attracts you.

3. Now draw out four or five major branches as thick lines radiating out from that central image. These branches could represent chapter headings, main themes or key questions or issues that the book or magazine raises.

4. Write a single word in CAPITALS above each branch that best describes the themes or ideas.

5. Draw thinner lines radiating from the thick lines to express any other associated ideas or thoughts you have.

6. Add creativity to your Mind Map through the use of symbols or simple pictures.

Mind Mapping was developed and popularised by Tony Buzan. Mind Map is a registered trade mark of the Buzan organisation.

EXAMPLE OF A HAND DRAWN MIND MAP

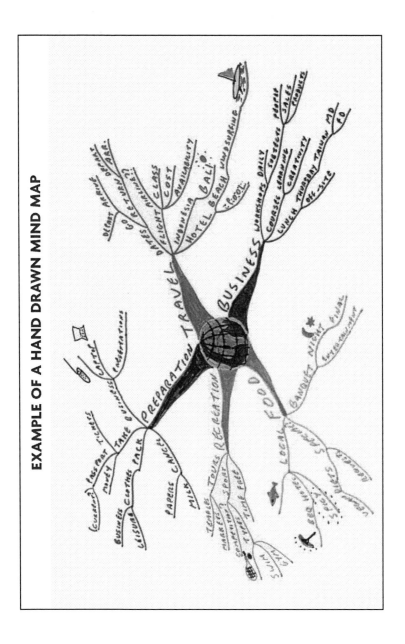

MIND MAP SKELETON. BUILD YOUR OWN LINKS
AND ASSOCIATIONS TO SUMMARISE THIS CHAPTER

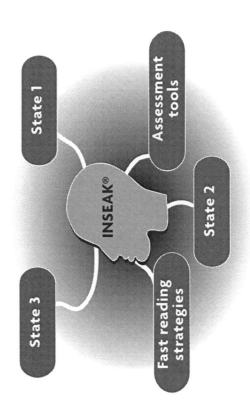

READING FASTER
WITH IMPROVED COMPREHENSION AND RECALL

The INSEAK approach is always extremely useful to have in mind when you have a new document to read. It allows you to assess information quickly so that you only have to read in detail those documents that you judge to be useful, relevant or appropriate.

That being said, however, I now want to put the INSEAK approach to one side and focus on what, for many people, is the essence of speed-reading – learning how to read much faster and discovering how to remember most, if not everything, they have read.

Now the usual objections around speed-reading concern comprehension. If, like Woody Allen, you speed-read War and Peace and can only remember that it is about Russia then that is a pretty poor result. Indeed, I would argue that there is absolutely no point in reading faster if you don't understand the content or if you are unable to recall the key information. However, the great surprise, and another key benefit of speed-reading, is the recognition that this is a process which actually helps you to remember more. It aids comprehension. How can this be?

The logic is as follows.

1. When we are reading slowly we typically stray from the text. We backtrack regularly and we also wander forward. Such wayward patterns of reading inevitably make it hard for us to follow the line of thought or logical argument put forward by the author. Indeed, when we read slowly we typically start

to listen to our own thoughts and ideas and can, on occasions, even start arguing with the focus or line of reasoning that the author is bringing. Such inner chatter is always distracting and impacts negatively on comprehension!

2. In contrast, speed-reading not only requires us to pay much more attention to finding meaning in the text but it also ensures that there is far less room for our own interruptions. This focus, and the speed at which we can progress, allows us to follow the themes in the article, document or book we are reading far better than before. Hence the inescapable conclusion that speed leads to increased comprehension.

3. When you speed-read you are gathering large chunks of information. This 'big picture' approach to reading business documents helps comprehension in the same way that having a picture on a puzzle helps you to make sense of the individual pieces.

4. In addition to this, speed-reading works on the basis that you probably already know quite a lot of information around the subject on which you are reading. In this respect you will be filling in the gaps as you go along.

So with all these arguments to back you up let us now find out how you can master this skill.

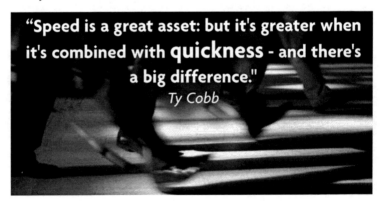

"Speed is a great asset: but it's greater when it's combined with **quickness** - and there's a big difference."
Ty Cobb

WHERE ARE YOU NOW?

The first step in reading faster is to know how fast you are already reading and in this respect there are two measures that I am going to ask you to consider – reading speed and reading comprehension. If you now turn to page 106 you will find an article entitled 'Silver Tongues and Fast Feet', which has been provided to help you in this regard. Remember that this is not a race. At this stage you are just trying to establish your current rate of reading. *So find a way to time yourself for just one minute, read normally and when your time is up then stop, mark the place you have reached and go to the end of the article* where you will be given some instructions about how to score yourself. When you are ready, begin.

So how far did you get? An average reading speed is around 240 words per minute, but don't be surprised if your total is different from this. On a typical workshop there is usually at least a 100% difference between the fastest and slowest reader in the group. To measure your personal speed, mark the place on the article which you had reached at the end of the allocated one minute. At the end of each paragraph you will find a word count figure that should help you. Total the number of words you have read in the paragraph where you finished and add it to the figure at the end of the previous para-

graph. The combined total is your current reading speed. Now make an estimate of how much of what you read you understood – this is your level of comprehension. Write down your scores below.

Reading exercise 1: Speed assessment

Current speed: words per minute _____

Current comprehension % _____

We will be repeating this exercise later on to see how much you manage to improve these figures – so let me now move onto the essential techniques that allow you to accelerate your reading speed.

ESTABLISHING A HIGHER BASE SPEED

There are four key techniques in speed-reading which can immediately help you to develop a much higher reading speed. These are bouncing, grouping, forward momentum and using a guide. All of these techniques need practice but if you follow my instructions closely you will find that you can make astonishing improvements in your reading speed in a very short period of time.

1. Bouncing

Before you start to read faster let me remind you how the eye and brain work. Remember that when we read our eyes make small jerky movements called saccades and the stop points between these movements are called fixations where we actually take in the information.

WHY READING SPEEDS VARY

We have been keeping records of reading speeds for around ten years and the average reading speed is consistent at 240 words per minute. However, the variation is considerable. So what are the factors that make such a difference? They are:

▶ the method that was used to teach us to read – usually either phonics, whole word or a hybrid system

▶ how much we enjoyed reading when we were young (including how much encouragement we received)

▶ how much reading we actually did when we were young

▶ the dominant type of reading we do now

▶ our enjoyment of, and attitude to, reading and especially the balance between reading for pleasure and other types of reading.

STACCATO vs LEGATO

The musical term, staccato, is comparable to bouncing. Staccato is the style of playing that sounds as though the payer is jumping from one note, or series of notes, to another. It contrasts with legato, which is the sound of smooth, flowing playing.

Now the point to note here is that most of us spend up to 20 times more time on these fixations than we need to. So if you can get faster at moving your eyes along the line then this will make a massive difference to your speed.

How do you do this? The trick is to start bouncing your eyes off the words as quickly as possible – literally from one word to the next. You will be doing this quite naturally when you are reading an exciting story and may well have experienced that feeling of jumping through the text. Now is the time to use that skill more consciously.

At the end of the next described technique I am going to ask you to practise this skill of bouncing. But take note ... in this initial phase of practice you may conclude that you are not taking in everything you are reading. Initially this may well be so but once you have learned the technique and established the habit, your comprehension will be completely restored.

2. Grouping

The second technique which you will learn to combine with bouncing is how to group words together.

When you first learned to read you mastered the process by vocalising the individual letters, then the syllables and then the single words. At a later date there came a moment when you were told by your teacher to just read in your head. This you did - but you probably continued to read one word at a time and also probably continued to 'hear' the words in your head. Indeed many adults still move their lips when they read – a sure sign that they are still sub-vocalising. There is nothing wrong with this but if this is your reading strategy then it will ensure that you are reading slowly.

In fact we know that the brain is capable of taking many words together with each fixation. In the same way that you understand a word without having to examine each letter, so you can expand your field of vision to take in two words, then three and then more. It will take practice but if you follow this technique where you learn to group words together you will soon find that your brain is able to make perfect sense of whole lines, sentences and even paragraphs on each single fixation.

Reading exercise 2: Bouncing and grouping

Go to the place you had reached in the article 'Silver Tongues and Fast Feet' and now read using these bouncing and grouping techniques together. Remember that you are

- trying to let your eyes bounce off the words

- trying to allow yourself to read whole phrases at a time

Again allow yourself one minute and score your speed and comprehension.

Reading score

New speed: words per minute   _____

New comprehension %   _____

3. A master of momentum

Most readers spend around 15% of their time re-reading words, paragraphs or whole pages

You may also be aware when you are reading that you sometimes have a tendency to re-read the sentence or paragraph that you have just read. The reason you do this is to reassure yourself that you have not missed or misunderstood anything important. However, research has shown that more than 90% of all such back-tracking is unnecessary in so far as it makes no difference to the overall understanding of what you have read.

The request I am making of you here, therefore, is that when you have the desire to go back over something you have just read, don't! Instead, keep reading forward and building up your momentum. It may feel uncomfortable at first but you will quickly find that once you have established a mastery of momentum – including bouncing and grouping words together – your reading will be far faster and more productive.

More than this, such forward momentum will also help with your levels of comprehension. Just consider … your current strategy is to keep on skipping back, re-reading paragraphs and perhaps even whole pages. This approach, where you keep on interrupting the flow, inevitably affects the logic and structure of what you are reading. In contrast, forward movement ensures that you keep up with the meaning of the text.

4. Using a guide

Using a guide such as a pencil, a finger or a cursor is an extra technique for speed-readers – and one that can help dramatically with momentum. In brief, a guide will help you to keep your eye moving smoothly along the  page. It will also reduce any wandering or back-skipping tendencies that you have.

The way you use a guide is to place it beneath the words you are reading and keep it gliding along the page in a continuous fashion, without stopping. You set the pace and allow your eye to follow.

Now for most speed-readers who are just starting out, the notion of using a guide can come as quite a shock. If this feels to you like going back to primary school then you need to re-frame this technique. Think of your guide as your pace-setter. It constantly leads you forward and keeps you focused. Indeed for some applications you are probably already using a guide. For example, what happens if you are adding up a column of figures? Or what occurs when you are trying to find a name in a phone directory or looking up a word in a dictionary? Typically in all these situations you will be using your finger as the guide – and all I am asking is that you extend this skill.

So remember … just take your pen or pencil and allow your eyes to follow the motion as you run it along the line. And trust me, your eye will be pulled along, drinking up the information on the page as you proceed at a pace which is already much faster than your normal reading speed.

Reading exercise 3: Using a guide

Go again to one of the articles in the appendices and practise this technique of using a guide.

Remember to time yourself for just one minute and when that one minute is finished total up your new reading score and write it down in the box below. And also estimate your level of comprehension when using a guide.

Reading score

New speed: words per minute   _____

New comprehension %   _____

IMPROVED COMPREHENSION AND RECALL

I have commented already that your comprehension will increase 'ine with your reading speed and and, of course, some people nd this hard to believe. As you are now in the territory of 'e theory into practice let me address this issue head on.

'hen you start using these speed-reading techniques 'our performance that your levels of comprehension may drop off. For some people this does occur. But if this happens to you do not be concerned. You are developing a new technique and the initial unfamiliarity might well get in the way of your learning. You need to practise for at least a week to start to build a new pattern (and three weeks to really establish it). That is the process of your brain establishing a new neural pathway – and the more you practise the stronger that pathway will become.

Better comprehension will also help with recall but there are other factors at work here too. One of the demands that speed-reading makes of its practitioners is that they become far more interactive in the process of reading. We can see this, for example, in terms of

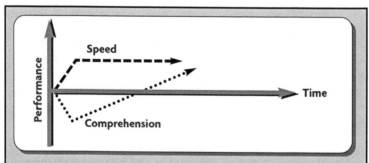

The initial relationship between speed and comprehension

Initially when we choose to read in a different way much of our conscious attention is on the technique and often we hear a 'voice' in our heads repeating the instructions to us – 'bounce the eyes, group the words, keep going forward'. Inevitably this concentration on the *process* is at the expense of the *content* and comprehension can then suffer.

This is why consistent practice is so important. As you get used to reading in the new way, less of your conscious attention will be on the process and more will be on the content. Your comprehension will then recover. For some this starts to happen very quickly; for others it takes a little longer.

speed-readers deciding how deeply they need to read a particular document or book and about the reading speed that is appropriate for any given piece of reading material.

In addition to this, there are those interactive techniques that help with comprehension and recall which I have already touched upon. Highlighting, underlining and annotating as you go along are techniques that all help to focus the mind – enabling you to recall information later on because you have visually encoded it.

The second aspect that helps with recall is to emphasise again that speed-reading requires an effective reviewing strategy such as Mind Mapping.

The reasons to review are compelling. Reviews enable you both to check your understanding of the material you have just read and to compress information into a visual format which will help enormously for later recall. However, as well as suggesting that you review your information by drawing up a Mind Map at the end of every reading assignment, I am also advising that you review your learning by looking at your Mind Maps on a regular basis.

Ideally, and this is especially so for anyone engaged in revision for professional examinations, a Mind Map review should take place one day, one week, one month and four months after your initial reading assignment. And the way to add even more weight to your learning is to add additional thoughts and linkages about the subject as you review your map. This will keep all the information and data fresh in your mind. It will also prevent you from having to go over old ground and so is an extraordinarily time-efficient approach to acquiring new knowledge.

ʸING MOTIVATED

ᶯve only just begun to develop your speed-reading
ʻ if you have been practising the four essential
ᶯd in this chapter then you should already be

able to see a big acceleration in your reading speed. Often people have, by this stage, already doubled their rate of reading. You can do even better than this, however, and there are more techniques for you to try out in chapter 5. But here's the rub – unless you practise, daily, any initial improvement will fade away.

Remember what we talked about in chapter two – about how we install new habits and how we have to develop an interest in order to engage our commitment. Now it is your turn to try this out. Find a book or a magazine that you have wanted to read for a long time – in which you have a genuine interest – but make sure that it isn't critical to your work (we are only practising here) and use this as your material for your daily practice.

Your challenge is to stay motivated during this initial phase. It is all too easy to agree that it would be good to change but still do nothing about it. So how can you break this pattern?

Motivation is tied in with your vision, so always remember why you have chosen to learn how to speed-read and know exactly how it is going to help you. Have a picture in your mind of how life will be when you have learned this skill. Hear someone giving you the sort of message you want to hear. Get a sense of how good that will feel.

Remember also that speed-reading is not hard to learn and it does not take too much time. It just requires that you are committed and set a regular amount of time aside (about 10 to 20 minutes a day) for the next week or two. However, I know that there are some people who, despite their best intentions, will find it hard to practise; so if you need to power up your motivation then here are some of `e motivational techniques that I recommend to practitioners.

'otivation is tied in with your vision, so `s remember why you have chosen to learn to speed-read

"We are what we
repeatedly do.
Excellence
then,
is not an act,
but a habit"
Aristotle

MIND MAP SKELETON. BUILD YOUR OWN LINKS AND ASSOCIATIONS TO SUMMARISE THIS CHAPTER

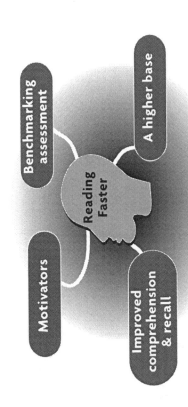

Benchmarking assessment

A higher base

Motivators

Reading Faster

Improved comprehension & recall

THE SEVEN MAGICAL MOTIVATORS

1. Use pain as the lever. Remember that pile of unfinished reading on your desk. Do you still want it to be there in a week, a month, a year? It will grow and cause you even more angst unless you make a change

2. Incentivise your learning. Reward yourself by giving yourself a real treat and/or a positive message before, and after, every practice session

3. Challenge your habit. Change requires you to run a new pattern and develop a new neural pathway. So don't get frustrated or depressed if you find that you have missed a practice session – get interested and curious in yourself

4. Tell someone whose opinion you really value, and who you do not want to let down, what you are going to do. Tell them why it matters to you and ask them to call you once a week for the next three weeks to see what progress you are making

5. Speak to someone else who has learned this skill and ask them how they did it. Model yourself on their ability to change

6. Keep on imagining yourself doing it. This isn't a joke ... your brain can't tell the difference between something you experience and something you imagine – and once you have established a pattern, even if it is only in your mind, it will become much easier to take action and make progress

7. Jump start it! Give yourself a really big reward for just starting the process. Think of something you really, really like ... and now find a way to multiply it. It's the jackpot principle and it can work extremely well when you are starting something new.

ADVANCED SPEED-READING TECHNIQUES

In this chapter I am going to explore ways in which you can read even faster by applying the most advanced speed-reading techniques. But before I do so, let me take a moment to remind you of some of the myths that have grown up around this subject and what the truth really is.

FALSE MYTHS

1. You may be able to read fast but you won't understand anything.
False. Increased reading speed actually increases your comprehension because it makes it easier to follow the structure of the text.

2. You may be able to read fast but you won't recall anything.
False . Speed-reading within the INSEAK approach is particularly designed to help you acquire knowledge and access that stored information when you need it.

3. Proper reading means focusing on every word.
False . The way to judge reading effectiveness is through reader understanding. In fact it has been estimated that up to 60% of the words on a page are neither critical nor important.

4. There are vital messages on every page.
False. Some writers use filler material and others repeat their messages or use unnecessary illustrations in order to try to bolster their argument. You will also find that some writing goes into far more detail then you need.

5. You can learn to speed-read in half an hour.
False . Speed-reading may be an accelerated learning technique but you still need to practise to become adept. However, with motivation and commitment, it is certainly true that it will not take you long to learn and it is definitely a worthwhile investment of your effort and time.

STRETCH GOALS

Remember what I said earlier. When you are about to try out new techniques you need to be clear about what you want and you need to be emotionally engaged in order to achieve your goals. The more intense your desire to achieve your outcome, the faster you are likely to get there. So how much faster do you want to go?

Now is the time to stretch yourself. Your goals should be both challenging and achievable. You know what your current reading speed is from the exercises you have gone through in this book and I hope you will also be practising regularly. So how much faster would you like to be able to read?

Wherever you are with your speed-reading practice, now is the time to check in with your purpose and intent. Where do you want to be in a week, in two weeks, a month? What would success look like to you? And will you know what that success is when it arrives? Remind yourself why you are making this effort and check your alignment by answering these questions.

- Do you know what you are doing this for?
- Have you chosen your attitude?
- Have you suspended any disbelief?
- Are you rested and alert?
- Have you eliminated all distractions?

Now it is time to get started. Choose reading material – articles, books or reports – with which you have some familiarity and some interest. But resist starting with that tempting pile of documents and magazines in your in-tray. Why? Because, as discussed in the previous chapter, during the early stages of learning to speed-read you will find that there is a trade-off between speed and comprehension. In other words, learn the skill first before applying it on your business-critical documents.

BUILDING UP YOUR SPEED

If you are one of those readers who want to achieve the fastest speeds possible, straight away, then fine – but remember that you will only succeed with speed-reading if you practise and master the four techniques we went through in the Reading Faster chapter. In addition to these, however, there are two other speed-reading techniques which can help you to accelerate further. These are learning how to build a faster average speed and peripheral reading.

Advanced technique 1: Establishing a higher average speed

The metaphor of driving is a useful one for speed-reading – especially in relation to how you can generate a faster average speed.

Let me start by recounting a short story which highlights how most of us manage our speed.

The first movie that Stephen Spielberg made, Duel, featured an anxious executive who was driving home – a long journey across state – when he found himself the target of a large tanker driven by an anonymous trucker with murderous intent. The executive, played by the actor Dennis Weaver, realised that if only he could overtake the tanker he would be able to escape this nightmare situation because his car was far faster, especially when going up hills.

Eventually Weaver managed to overtake his tormentor and began to leave the truck behind. However, to his dismay, he then found that, despite himself, he settled back into his habitual 50mph comfort zone – and as soon as this happened the tanker driver started to catch up.

Now, in the film, Dennis Weaver never quite manages to escape from the trucker and there is, of course, a final confrontation. However, the learning I want to draw out of this story is that we all drive, and read, within a comfort zone. For short periods of time we may be able to adjust our speed but when the pressure is released we have a tendency to slip back again into our habitual way of being.

So how can we break this pattern? The answer to this conundrum is to practise reading at a speed which is two or three times your usual speed and, at the beginning, not to worry in the least about your levels of comprehension.

Driving your reading speed up in this fashion will ensure that when you throttle back you will find that your average 'comfort' speed has increased. So, in other words, you need to drive regularly at 100mph in order to raise your 'comfort' speed from, say, 40mph to 60mph.

High speed reading exercise 3: Raising your comfort levels

1. Find a book or document that engages you and also choose a guide that works for you e.g. a pen or pencil.

2. Practise moving your guide at a rate that is faster than you would normally read. Make your eye chase the guide and trust that before too long you will be picking up the key words and themes of the text. After one minute check your reading speed and your comprehension.

Speed: words per minute _____

Comprehension %   _____

Advanced technique 2: Peripheral reading

Allied to the idea of grouping words (see page 51) is the notion of using your peripheral vision i.e. what you can see out of the corner of your eyes. And here I am talking both about what you can see horizontally as well as what you can see vertically.

Again the science backs us up here because up to 80 per cent of what you can see will be outside the area on which you are focusing. Your guide (finger or pencil) can help you too because the technique involved in peripheral reading is to change your habit from moving along the line to reading only the middle two-thirds of the page, letting your eyes pick up the words on the edge of the page as you scroll down.

Of course you already use this technique with driving. As a driver you will always be looking ahead – but at the same time you will be fully aware of key activity to your left and right. Just look at this picture of a road below. Your eyes don't only take in the lines on the road's surface but also the trees, the verge and the sky. You can use the same skills with reading. You just have to map this ability across to a new context.

Let me now outline three separate techniques which can help you to build up your peripheral reading skills. Some people may find that these techniques take a little bit of getting used to while others may find that they are surprisingly familiar. My advice to you is to try them out and enjoy the stretch that they may present. In my experience many people find that they are able to develop their peripheral vision very quickly and find it to be a skill that complements previewing and skimming techniques.

"The secret of business is to
know something
that nobody else knows"
Aristotle Onassis

DEVELOP YOUR PERIPHERAL READING SKILLS

Open a book which you have to hand and, taking your guide, follow each line starting an inch in from the left margin and finishing an inch from the right margin i.e. you are focusing only on two thirds of each line. Run your guide along each line in this way trusting that your eye will pick up the words on the periphery of your vision.

Open a book that you have to hand and, taking your guide, follow each line starting an inch in from the left margin and finishing an inch from the right margin i.e. you are focusing only on two thirds of each line. Run your guide along each line in this way trusting that your eye will pick up the words on the periphery of your vision. Open a book an

Once you have practised the technique, above, there are two further steps you can take to build your reading speed. The first of these is to run your guide in a slow but smooth 'S' like motion down the page. This approach is faster still and relies even more on your peripheral vision.

Open a book that you have to hand and, taking your guide, follow each line starting an inch in from the left margin and finishing an inch from the right margin i.e. you are focussing only on two thirds of each line. Run your guide along each line in this way trusting that your eye will pick up the words on the periphery of your vision. Open a book an

And even faster than this, and once you know that the above process works, you can imagine that there is a line running right down the middle of the page which you follow with your guide. This may feel a big step to take but, with practice, you can train your mind to read on 'both sides of the road' even though your eyes are on the centre of the page.

Open a book that you have to hand and, taking your guide, follow each line starting an inch in from the left margin and finishing an inch from the right margin i.e. you are focussing only on two thirds of each line. Run your guide along each line in this way trusting that your eye will pick up the words on the periphery of your vision. Open a book an

MIND MAP SKELETON. BUILD YOUR OWN LINKS AND ASSOCIATIONS TO SUMMARISE THIS CHAPTER

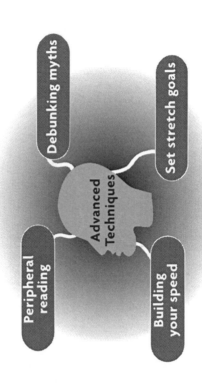

Advanced Techniques

Debunking myths

Set stretch goals

Peripheral reading

Building your speed

FLEXING SPEED & DEPTH

We have now looked at both the essential and the advanced speed-reading techniques and it is time to reconsider the relevance of the INSEAK approach to speed. Remember that the INSEAK approach is based on the principle that when we read for information and knowledge we always need to be assessing our material. In an age of information overload, 'time' and 'efficiency' are the commodities that we are most concerned with here.

LEARNING TO FLEX

When it comes to reading, the question of what speed you want to travel at is one that you should always keep in mind.

It is my experience that people who try to speed-read everything, indiscriminately, are often the first to lose motivation. It is as if they forget to exercise choice or ignore the fact that they have

both an accelerator and a brake. So don't fall into this trap and remember that while some documents need to be read fast there are others that can be read slowly and some which don't need to be read at all. Remember the example of the visitor to the art gallery? When they realised that there were no paintings in the gallery that they particularly wanted to study, they had a choice – to leave immediately or to take some time to walk around and see if there was anything else that they might enjoy looking at.

Let me expand on this because there is an important principle at stake here.

When I am reading for pleasure, I prefer to read slowly. This isn't so for everyone. You have probably met people in your life who read novels extraordinarily quickly. It's simply a matter of choice. To continue the driving metaphor we need to be able to vary our driving speed. If you are in a beautiful part of the country, or when you have time to spare, you may want to take it slowly. On motorways, or when time is pressing, you may want to accelerate.

This variable speed approach is especially relevant for those executives for whom the acquisition of information and knowledge is a pressing need. The INSEAK approach is underpinned by continuous assessment but it also requires your ability to flex. In other words you need to know what strategies and speeds you need for different types of reading material. Flexing is all about understanding that such differences exist and applying yourself accordingly.

As to how to assess and flex when you are speed-reading, here are the key principles to consider.

1. Flexing your priorities

Assessment is the 'big chunk' approach to flexing. We have already looked at the initial evaluation technique in chapter 3, a process which can help you to identify the relevance of any document in just a few minutes. But how do you determine relevance? Here are some key criteria which might prove useful.

> ▶ Determine importance. What 'must' you read, what do you feel you 'should' read and what only needs a cursory overview? It is often the 'should' read pile that you will find needs most of your attention because we tend to accumulate a number of books, magazines and documents that we feel we 'should' read but never get around to opening. Get clear about how many of them you actually 'must' read and reduce your in-tray.

> ▶ Decide on delegation. Some documents can be handed on. Be

aware that some material might be better read by someone else. You don't need to know everything.

▶ Assess the urgency. Does the document that you have decided is a priority need your immediate attention or can it be left until you have more time later, tomorrow or even next week?

2. Flexing around purpose

When you are clear what you are looking for, and what you want to get out of the time you are spending on reading, then make sure you set the appropriate reading pace. For example, compare the approach you might take when you are browsing an industry publication with the in-depth study you might need to do on a new product or service brochure. Knowing why you are reading, and how much detail you need to go into, will help you to determine how much time you need and at what speed you need to read.

3. Flexing around the detail

Even when you have decided you must read a document or report does that mean you have to read all of it? Almost certainly not. Give yourself permission to skim through some sections where you know the arguments, or are familiar with the terrain, and slow down in others where you want more thinking time. If, for example, you only need to know what conclusions the author comes to, then go straight to that section of the proposal or report.

It is especially worth remembering that many books, magazines and reports share a common structure. They have sections which are information-rich and sections which might be described as padding. For books in particular the typical format to bear in mind is that:

▶ the first chapter typically sets out the framework for the book and how ideas and arguments are going to be presented

▶ the last chapter typically summarises and draws together the findings, suggests next steps and highlights actions.

This same pattern may also be repeated in the individual chapters within a book. A preview is contained within the first few paragraphs and a summary is contained at the end of a chapter. So if you do not want, or need, to read at greater depth this provides you with a way of gleaning the information you need in a very short time.

Finally with flexing, remember that you have brakes and must be prepared to use them. With speed-reading you can get through material at an extremely rapid rate but there are traps for the unwary. For example, when you come to unfamiliar terminology, difficult sentence structure or unfamiliar concepts then it is time to slow down. Indeed if you are reading technical material it is often a good idea to take a couple of minutes just to see whether the author has given a brief definition of new concepts or abbreviations that s/he has used.

CLEAR YOUR DESK

For some people having a large stack of unread material on their desk can cause considerable stress. If that is the case for you then here is an approach designed to help:

1. Assess each document on your desk based solely on its front and back cover and contents page. Be clear that the purpose of this exercise is to create three piles - a 'must read' pile, a 'ditch' pile (put these documents straight into the waste basket) and a 'not sure' pile.

2. Now assess the 'not sure' pile by skimming each document for context and/or scanning it for particular information. Be ready to ditch anything that doesn't meet your criteria. Also be ready to cut out articles from magazines that you want to keep and so create a knowledge file.

3. Now assess the 'must read' pile and prioritise these in terms of must read today, this week or some time in the future. File the some time in the future pile and diarise 'essential reading' time.

Additionally it is worth emphasising that even within those business related documents that fall into the 'sprint read' category there will be certain chapters or passages which may require you to slow down. Be prepared for this. You are the driver and you need to be able to make decisions about your speed as you go along. It is this ability to adjust that will determine whether you become an effective or ineffective speed-reader.

Just as with driving a car, you will find that at the beginning there appears to be a lot to work out – but you will soon find that you are going through the gears without thinking about it. It will all quickly become second nature. Just keep on practising and you will find that you develop a range of speeds depending on the type of road you are on.

HOW DO YOU KNOW WHEN TO SPEED UP AND WHEN TO SLOW DOWN?

You may want to slow down your reading speed if

▶ you are reading for pleasure
▶ you feel like it
▶ the ideas are difficult (but worth it)
▶ the ideas you are reading especially interest you
▶ there is technical jargon which you don't know

You may want to increase your reading speed if

▶ you know the topic area
▶ you are reading for information
▶ you want an overview
▶ there are illustrations or graphics which repeat the messages in the text
▶ there is unnecessary detail

EXTRA LEVERAGE FOR FORMAL LEARNING

The INSEAK approach is an ideal structure for anyone who has formal learning requirements because it helps you to assess, prioritise, read, understand and recall key information.

The approach outlined on the page opposite requires you to be an active participant in your learning and in this respect you need to be as clear as possible about your objectives and the information you are looking for, before you start reading.

The approach also requires that you know how to Mind Map so if this is a section of the book that you have skipped over then please re-read it. The relevant pages are 41-45 and if you want more information on this technique you can go to www.mind-mapping.com.

As for the approach itself, you will see that I have divided it into two parts – planning and action. Many of us tend to rush the planning part of learning because we feel we are wasting time and want to immerse ourselves in the detail. If that is your tendency then now is the time to restrain yourself. This approach depends on your ability to break old habits and behave in ways that may be unfamiliar but which I predict will help you to achieve outstanding results.

"Over the long run superior **performance** depends on superior learning"

Peter Senge

MULTI-LAYERED STUDYING APPROACH

The INSEAK approach provides the underpinning tools and techniques you need for formal learning. Use this process to consider how you might proceed with a piece of formal study.

Plan it

▶ Set clear objectives. Be clear about how much time you have to study, the amount you have to cover and the breaks you will need.

▶ Mind Map what you already know about the topic of the book you are studying. This sharpens your mind and prepares the brain to attach the new information to that you already have, thereby aiding your understanding and memory.

▶ Conduct a rapid pre-read of your book. View every page and mark the sections that engage you. Don't go over those areas that you already know, sections which are weak or material that doesn't apply. Choose to spend your time on areas which are important.

▶ Edit your Mind Map. See if there are any key themes or associated ideas you want to add to your Mind Map.

Action it

▶ Pre-read the book again with all the clarity you now have. Pay particular attention to results, conclusions, tables, statistics, sub-headings, dates, italics, capitalised words and graphs.

▶ Skim read. This time cover all the information not covered in the Rapid pre-read. Focus especially on beginnings and ends of paragraphs, sections and chapters. And also pay particular attention to summaries and conclusions.

▶ Speed-read and review. If you still need more information then speed-read the relevant parts of the book. If further reading is required then do it now. Make sure that problem areas are solved and questions answered. Build your Mind Map as you are progressing and use the Mind Map as your review vehicle for the following days and weeks.

MIND MAP SKELETON. BUILD YOUR OWN LINKS
AND ASSOCIATIONS TO SUMMARISE THIS CHAPTER

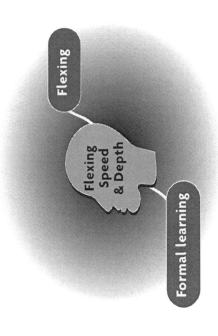

MANAGE YOUR LEARNING STATE

If your objective in reading is to relax, or be entertained, then you will bring your own personal attitude and state that will enable you to achieve this outcome. However, the focus in this book is on being able to manage information and acquire new knowledge and this will require a quite particular state of readiness. So how can this be achieved?

Let me start this enquiry by asking a question about how you are, right now.

How would you describe your state, at this very moment, as you are reading this page? Are you curious or expectant? Or, on the other hand, are you in a more detached state?

Your state is 'your way of being' which includes how you are thinking and feeling, and how much physical energy you have. Some states are pleasant, some are not. And more to the point, some are useful and some are not. In this context, the state you are in when you sit down to speed-read will impact directly on how ready you are to take in new knowledge and information. That is why it is important both to be aware of your state and to discover how you can manage it.

Your state will vary from day to day and sometimes even from minute to minute. If you doubt this then just remember how it can affect you when someone tells you what a great person you are, or how well you have done on a particular project. In contrast, consider how it felt last time when you felt that you had failed with a particular initiative or you received some critical feedback.

The truth is that your state can, and often does, change regularly – but it is also the case that you will have an 'at home' state that will be very familiar to you. To find out what yours is just complete this simple exercise over the page.

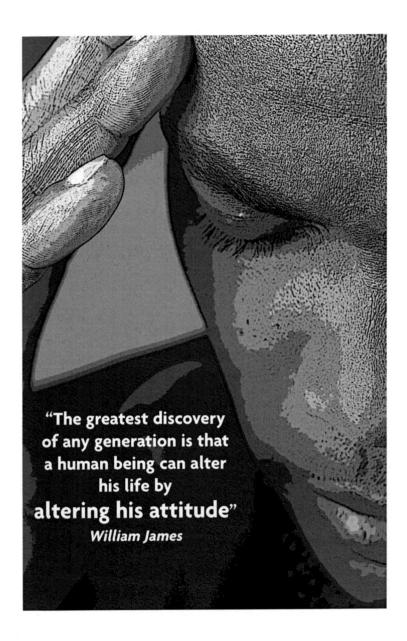

"The greatest discovery of any generation is that a human being can alter his life by **altering his attitude**"
William James

Exercise on your 'at home' state

Take a moment and think about what it is like when you are in a typical 'at home' state. You may be able to describe this state immediately but, if not, then here are some useful ways to gather information about this way of being.

▶ Consider your body and your health. How much energy do you normally have? How light or heavy do you feel? How comfortable or tense are you in your body? How would someone describe what it is like being around you?

▶ Now think about your mind. Are you always planning ahead or thinking about the past? Are you always hard driving or are you quite relaxed? How active are you in your thinking?

▶ How would you characterise your feeling state? Are you 'happy go lucky' or typically more anxious about what tomorrow may bring? What colour would you associate with your emotions?

▶ And finally what about your spiritual state? How connected are you to a sense of purpose or meaning? How inspired are you?

With all this information now take a moment to describe your 'at home' state in one sentence and/or with one image.

Describe your 'at home' state

_____

_____

_____

Do you have an image for your 'at home' state?

_____

_____

Of course there are no rights or wrongs with whatever answer you came up with. This is just information. However, it does provide clues as to why state management is important. If, for example, in your 'at home' state you are always pushing, or always anxious, then this is unlikely to be a productive learning state. So this leads onto the next question, namely, what would be the best state for learning and how can you develop such a state?

SIX STATE REGULATORS

It is clear that our ability to learn is 'state dependent' – so let me now highlight six key factors that can help you to access the most positive learning state available to you:

1. Outcome: knowing what you want

When it comes to speed-reading you need to start by knowing what you want to get out of the time and attention you are investing in

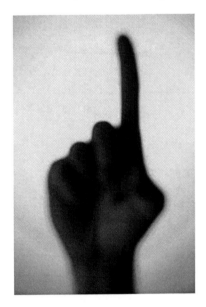

"I was going to buy a copy of 'The power of positive thinking' and then I thought 'What the hell good would that do?"
Ronnie Shakes
US humourist

this approach. For some speed-readers this is simple to answer; they are under increasing pressure to get through vast amounts of material every day and INSEAK offers them a way to manage this situation. For other people the objective might be to satisfy their appetite for new knowledge. Whatever your challenge, it is vital that you know why you are learning this technique and what you want to get from it.

Complementing this, it is extraordinarily helpful when you know what the specific benefits are that you are going to derive from using INSEAK and speed-reading. Some people may want to use this approach as a daily practice – for example in getting through their in-tray faster than before. But for other people there may be a particular project for which INSEAK is appropriate. For instance, if you are studying towards professional qualifications or examinations, or you know that, in some way, what you are reading could have a direct impact on your career. In such cases INSEAK is an ideal learning strategy.

When you are in touch with the benefits of absorbing new information, and recognise that INSEAK is the right tool for the job, then this will strengthen your resolve and set you up in a way that is powerfully aligned with your objectives.

2. Attitude: Choosing your approach

In addition to being clear about your outcome, you also need to consider the way in which you are approaching the task of reading your document, report or book. Before you sit down what is your attitude towards this endeavour? Are you fully and positively engaged, or are you approaching the reading in front of you with a heavy heart or even deep frustration?

It is no surprise to find that if you sit down thinking that what you are about to read is going to be dull and time consuming then it will be so. The attitude that you bring to your work will reinforce your beliefs. So how can you generate open-mindedness and a positive attitude towards reading?

"No person who is enthusiastic about his work has anything to fear from life"
Samuel Goldwyn

The answer to this is simple. First of all identify a quality that you think will help you get into the state you want to be in and then use the following technique to resource yourself.

Exercise: Powering up your attitude

i) Draw an imaginary circle on the floor – don't step into it yet – and think about the reading you need to do, your objectives, the time you have available to speed-read and the state you are currently in.

ii) Now think of three qualities that would help you to have a positive attitude. For example 'interest' and 'enjoyment' could be such qualities.

iii) Step into the circle and think yourself back to a time when you know you had the first of these qualities i.e. when you were interested. Remember what you were doing and how it felt when you were 'interested'. When you have re-lived that experience step out of the circle. (Repeat this same process for the other two qualities).

iv) Step into the circle again and now consider your present situation. And in your mind's eye bring towards you each one of the qualities you've identified. Do this by breathing the qualities in, putting them on like a coat or digesting them in a way that makes sense to you.

v) As you bring these qualities in to the present, notice how they infect your attitude and consider how they might influence your approach to the task of reading.

This process can be extremely helpful. All you have to do is search for times when you have had an experience of the quality you want to reproduce and practise stepping into it or putting it on. Sometimes this resourcing can feel like a physical action and the magic of this technique is that the very process of getting in touch with the state you want can itself be the outcome.

3. Belief: The art of possibility thinking

Everyone will have a set of beliefs about speed-reading. You may start with the belief that it is possible for you to speed-read a newspaper but still not believe that you can speed-read a proposal or a project report. Or you may believe that it is possible for others to speed-read, but not for you.

However, in the same way that you can choose your attitude, you can also install new beliefs that are consistent with your desires for speed-reading.

This process of managing beliefs starts with awareness. If you know that you are holding beliefs that are not consistent with your objective e.g. you don't believe it is possible to speed-read your way through all that information that lies on your desk, or which is stacked up in your computer, then guess what, for you it won't be.

The interesting finding about beliefs is that they tend to act as filters which predetermine our future. We act as if our beliefs are true when, quite frequently, they are not. So start by examining what you believe about speed-reading and consider whether that is a useful belief to hold. If you find that you are holding a belief which is not useful then just ask yourself whether you are willing to suspend that belief while you assess whether another belief might, for this task, be more helpful.

It is important to note that when you are working with beliefs you have to work with your own willingness to change. Some beliefs are tied up with your identity and this makes them very hard to shift. If you try to force-fit a new belief but it doesn't feel comfortable then nothing will change. 'I tried it, but it didn't work' would be a typical response for someone who is in this pattern.

In contrast, when you suspend disbelief and open up to new possibilities which might be articulated, for example, 'I believe that speed-reading could work for me' then it gives you room to try it out. And once you have proved to yourself that you can achieve your goal, your positive experience provides evidence for the shift in belief to become permanent.

4. Concentration: Working with the grain

Get to know how you work and learn best. This is a golden thread running throughout this chapter. For example, are you a morning person or an evening person? When do you need to eat and what food helps you to be alert? How much rest do you need to be at your best?

These questions are directly relevant to your concentration and your success as a speed-reader. However, they are not the only issues to consider here.

It is amazing to discover how many people, despite all evidence to the contrary, believe that they can maintain their concentration, hour after hour, and take in new information at a consistent rate throughout. It isn't possible. All the studies about how we learn have proven that when we take breaks, and look after ourselves, we are better able to take in new information. So here are three simple practices which I encourage you to use in order to help

both your concentration and effectiveness as a learner.

❱ Take regular, planned breaks. This will give your eyes and your mind time to re-charge. And during these breaks do something different. If you are really attuned you may want to do some meditation or use the eye exercises below.

❱ Make sure you drink water regularly – not just coffee and tea – and eat healthy, brain-rich foods such as fruit and salads and fish which are rich in Omega 3 fatty acids.

▶ Learn to stretch in order to increase circulation and, if you really want to treat yourself, give your eyes, temples, hands or fingers a gentle massage.

Pay attention to these three simple practices and you will notice an immediate improvement in your concentration.

EXERCISES TO RELIEVE EYE FATIGUE

▶ Change your focus. If you have been doing a lot of close-up reading then change your focus and look to the horizon. Notice what you can see, scan around you

▶ Palm your eyes. Rub your hands together until they are warm and then place your palms over your closed eyes. Notice the warmth as it filters into your eyelids and relaxes any strain you might have accumulated

▶ Move your eyes. Sit straight and gently move your eyes up to the ceiling and down to the floor. Do this movement slowly and several times. Then look from left to right, focusing as far to each side as you can manage without moving your head. Now circle the eyes and see if you can achieve a nice easy and smooth rotation

▶ Massage. Place your forefinger and your middle finger on your temples and lightly make small rotational movements. See if you can smooth away any furrows in your brow and gently stretch the skin around the corners of your eyes. Breathe out any stress.

5. Relaxed attentiveness: The alpha state

As I have already suggested, the whole brain is necessary for learning. This includes your ability to engage the 'left brain' (which works well with numbers, words, lists and logic) and the 'right brain' (with its capacity for colour, rhythm, space, imagination and overviewing). And when you are using both hemispheres you increase your ability to access the so-called alpha state.

The alpha state can be measured by studying the electrical current and waves in the brain and can be characterised as a state of 'relaxed attentiveness'. In this state we know that the following things occur – there is increased co-ordination between the two hemispheres of the brain, there is greater access to the middle part of the brain (the limbic system) and there is increased production of gamma amino butyric acid, the neurotransmitter that helps us to block out unwanted stimuli.

Some people find it easy to move into this state, while others find it more difficult. However, the following practices have all been found to facilitate this state – meditation, brain gym (physical exercises designed to co-ordinate the brain), Yoga and listening to non-choral music of the same tempo as the brain waves.

Some of these practices may be familiar to you, others may not, but the concept of stimulating your mind in a way which complements your learning objectives is certainly one that can help your state.

6. Environment: Managing the external

Finally, there is the question of your external learning environment. Do you learn well when you are on the move? Are you likely to take in information when there is a lot of noise going on all around you? How about when it's too hot, too cold or when there isn't enough light?

You get the point. Your learning state will be impacted by the conditions in which you are trying to learn. So clearly there is a major benefit in managing your external environment. In this context here are some of the key factors to consider:

❱ Does your environment have natural lighting?

❱ Is the temperature comfortable for you?

❱ Do you need fresh air?

❱ What noise is likely to distract you – and can you lessen its impact?

❱ Is your chair comfortable and is your office an environment in which you want to learn?

❱ Do you have easy access to other resources that you may need while you are speed-reading e.g. pens or paper?

There is also one other consideration – developing a sensory-rich environment in which to learn. Let us imagine that all the above conditions have been met and that you are on your own in a comfortable, but extremely uniform, white office. Such a room might be suitable for a short project but actually the brain works best when it is stimulated. That is why children's classrooms are usually a riot of colour and imagination. People respond well to such stimuli so here is your challenge … do what you can to make your learning environment one that is inspirational, one that engages your creative mind and is conducive to learning.

And finally remember that there is always a social element to learning and there is nothing like having someone with whom you can share new knowledge to enhance your state and stimulate your thinking.

So do you have a colleague with whom you can talk about your new ideas? Or are there opportunities for you to discuss what you have just read with friends or family? The important point to note is that your sharing of new information with others will help you to install it and will also help you when you want to recall it. So be on the look out for ways to engage others with your newly learned ideas and insights.

MIND MAP SKELETON. BUILD YOUR OWN LINKS
AND ASSOCIATIONS TO SUMMARISE THIS CHAPTER

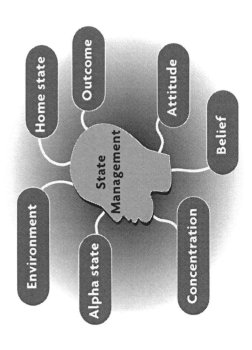

FINAL WORD

So, are you ready to become an extraordinary reader? For those of you who can't wait, the next step is to start practising and building your confidence in the various tools and techniques which make up the INSEAK approach. However, before you begin, let me summarise the advice and information that I have provided in this book and re-emphasise exactly what this process will require from you.

ENGAGE WITH YOUR PURPOSE

If you are embarking on the journey to become an extraordinary reader then you need to be absolutely clear about your purpose. What do you want from this process? I have suggested that your outcomes will probably have little to do with achieving a specific reading speed and more to do with improving your ability to manage information and acquire new knowledge. However, you may well want to become more focused than this and, if so, then now is the time to set your objective.

The outcome(s) that I want to achieve are:

1. _____

2. _____

3. _____

These outcomes not only provide you with a clear goal, they will help you to stay motivated and will provide much-needed momentum for your learning. In this respect I urge you to ensure that your outcomes are both appropriate and are enough of a stretch for you. The investment in time and energy that you are making has to be worth your while, so make sure that what you want will make a significant difference to your working life.

BRING YOUR POSITIVE BEST

When you are learning any new skill you need to start with, and maintain, a positive attitude and this means ensuring that your beliefs are in line with what you want. If you examine your beliefs and find that you don't think your outcome is achievable, then you have two choices. The first is to suspend your disbelief and act 'as if' what you are aiming for is quite within your reach. In this way you can build evidence of success as you make progress without any of your limiting beliefs getting in your way.

The alternative is to change your limiting beliefs. Most of us act as if our beliefs are absolute truths – but they are not. And at any time you can decide to hold a new belief. The point to underline here is that beliefs drive behaviour, so if you find that you are holding a limiting belief (e.g. I don't believe speed-reading will work for me) then this will prevent you from achieving the outcome you want. You can find out more about how to change beliefs on page 84 but in essence the requirement is to develop a new empowering belief that is aligned with the objective you have set (e.g. speed-reading will help me to read faster, understand better and remember more).

Generating positive beliefs ensures that you have the right foundations, but you also need to bring a constructive learning state to your task. Chapter seven focuses on state management and core to this topic is the understanding that you can choose the way in which you approach learning. What is your best state? It is probably associated with being curious, open-minded and interested and you need to ensure that you bring this 'state' to bear every time you sit down to practise being an extraordinary reader.

INSTALL NEW HABITS

It is important to note that speed-reading will not stop you from enjoying those books or documents that you want to read slowly.

BEING AN EXTRAORDINARY READER
- THE ESSENTIALS -

▶ Know exactly why you want to speed-read

▶ Be prepared to change your reading habits

▶ Develop an understanding of how you learn

▶ Consider what is your most resourceful learning state

▶ Bring a positive attitude to the task

▶ Make sure you are not obstructed by self-limiting beliefs

▶ Build a better understanding of ways to improve recall

▶ Practise the INSEAK techniques on non-essential reading material

▶ Remember to be flexible in your approach

▶ Reward yourself for your progress

In this context I am suggesting that you should not be trying to eliminate the reading strategy that you have been using successfully for many years. Rather, I am proposing that you should be looking to develop an additional and complementary reading habit that you can use when and where you need it.

So how do you install a new habit? You have to practise, that is all. And it will only take you about three weeks before you have mastered this skill and developed a new neural pathway. Once this habit is installed you can then flex as required – speeding up or slowing down depending on the nature of the material and your objectives.

But remember. When you start it is not recommended that you immediately practise on important work-related documents. Build up your skills by practising on non-essential reading material before you start applying yourself to business-critical information.

ASSESS CONTINUOUSLY

INSEAK has power as a framework because it invites you to have in mind at all times what you are looking for, and what you want to extract, from the document you are reading.

In this process continuous assessment is the key.

You do not need to read every page of every document that comes across your desk. That would be a complete waste of your time. Instead you can use INSEAK to evaluate new documents, assess new information and build your knowledge quickly and efficiently.

Looked at in a different way, although INSEAK helps you to acquire and assimilate information, it does not require you to slavishly follow a rigid process. On the contrary, you can enter and exit from the INSEAK approach at any time. When you have sufficient information or knowledge from the document you are reading you can simply move on.

DEVELOP YOUR FLEXIBILITY

There is a tension for many people who suffer from information overload between getting through all the material that arrives on their desks and comprehending the content of those documents that they have to read. INSEAK helps to address this issue.

The techniques described in this book not only help readers to make quick evaluations of the relevance of new information to their work, they also provide readers with a way to double or triple their reading speed. And in addition to this they help readers to understand better, and recall more of, what they are reading.

However, INSEAK requires readers to be flexible. This isn't a 'one speed suits all' approach to reading. In addition to using continuous assessment to evaluate relevance, INSEAK emphasises that there are a range of high-speed reading techniques which you can use within any particular reading project. So as well as applying the fast reading strategies of skimming, scanning and speed-reading to your projects, the challenge for extraordinary readers is to be able to slow down or speed up in the moment, as required.

AND FINALLY ... ENJOY IT

I have a belief that reading is enjoyable. And more than this, I also believe that the process of becoming an extraordinary reader is extremely worthwhile. So I encourage you to make the learning of this method into a delight. To support this I recommend you follow these three simple guidelines:

- make sure that you are interested in what you read
- remember to reward yourself for the progress you make and
- notice the benefits to your working life as you begin to master this extraordinary approach.

The following pages provide sample articles on which to practise your speed-reading. As an aid you will find a word count at the end of each paragraph. This is to help you to evaluate how fast you are reading.

There is too much business writing that is long-winded, impenetrable and filled with meaningless jargon. You see it every day in emails, in direct mail and on web sites. But the people writing this gobbledegook are trying hard to communicate effectively. So why are they getting it so wrong? In this article Anthony Landale looks at the issue of how poor writing continues to plague business and considers what can be done about it. (75)

CUTTING THE BULL

How often have you read reports, policies or documents which, however hard you try, simply fail to make sense? You aren't alone; indeed there is even an annual award for the most baffling of these texts – The Golden Bull Award – and, as you will see in panel 1 at the end of this article, this year's winner is an absolute peach. (139)

But however entertaining it may be to poke fun at corporate gobbledegook, there is real problem here. Just consider the fact that only 10–15% of what you and your team put in your proposals, reports, letters, emails and brochures ever gets read. Why? Well don't blame the reader. Who, for example, would want to read this twaddle from an NHS Trust … "Where the combined value of the above payments before actual assimilation remains greater than the combined value of the payments after assimilation, the former level of pay will be protected. These protection arrangements apply to the combined value of payments before and after assimilation, not to individual pay components, excepting the provision relating to retention of existing on-call arrangements."(261)

It's bewildering isn't it? However, the real irony is that the people writing this sort of nonsense are trying very hard to communicate effectively. OK, they are failing miserably, but the answer is not for them to stop trying. Rather, the solution is for them to learn key skills that can transform this rubbish into clear, persuasive and engaging writing.(321)

Some organisations, of course, recognise the negative impact that poor or impenetrable writing has on those people who have to read it and have started to take steps to address this situation. The City of Edinburgh Council is one such example, as senior consultant at the Council, Pat Angus, explained. "We write and publish reports, plans and policies all the time, and increasingly these are available on our web site, so it is important for the public who want to access them that they are clear and easy to understand. (411)

"However, despite our best intentions, we know that we are sometimes unnecessarily long-winded and that we can improve our performance. So with this in mind we have been looking at how we can train our managers to improve their standard of writing." (453)

It is interesting to note that Pat Angus went through a rigorous process to find a supplier who could help the Council. The organisation already had two existing writing courses available to managers but she wanted something that significantly raised their game and decided that they needed extra help from a specialist consultancy. (506)

But how can you differentiate between one expert supplier and another? After an extensive trawl through the various options, the only course that Pat Angus felt matched her needs was the award-winning programme, Writing Dynamics which is provided by the accelerated learning specialists, illumine Training. (553)

This course starts from the premise that anyone can learn to write well so long as a) they have a spoken command of the language and b) they follow a system. Moreover, this course addresses that key concern about effectiveness – it does not attempt to turn business writers into novelists; rather it aims to help busy professionals improve the quality of their writing – and to do so fast! (625)

The writing system around which this course is based concerns the three basics – planning, drafting and editing - and what is an immediate wake-up call for all participants is to find that they spend much too much time writing. Professional writers spend twice as much time in the planning and less than half the time in the drafting of text compared to non-professionals. So let us now focus on each of these three phases of Writing Dynamics and pull out some of the distinctive elements involved. (709)

Planning productively

The first stage in any planning process is to organise your ideas on paper much faster. (728)

In this context there are a number of powerful planning techniques which you can use. Mind Mapping is one and you can find out more about how to use this planning tool on www.mind-mapping.com. Another is the 'cluster' technique which, like Mind Mapping, allows you to put down on one page all the various associated thoughts that you have around your subject. Both these techniques help you to:

– show the whole subject at once

– see the relationship between ideas

– beat writer's block

– avoid worries about grammar, punctuation and spelling

– develop creativity (824)

In essence, these techniques help you to brainstorm the subject, to prioritise the various elements that need covering and then to structure them into a logical order. However, the organising strategies which participants may wish to impose on their writing still allow for individuality. For example, some people may group their ideas into an order of importance, into a 1–2–3 sequence.

Others, especially when it comes to a schedule or planning procedure, might choose a chronological plan e.g. here we are now, this is what we are planning to do and this is where we will end up. Alternatively, the How, What, Who, Where, When and Why approach allows the writer to cover all the bases when trying to write a report or set out a proposal. (952)

The fast draft

The planning process of any writing project should probably take about 40% of your time whereas the drafting stage of writing should only take about 25% – so how do professional writers write so fast? (989)

What Writing Dynamics teaches are the following principles:

– Begin anywhere

– Write rough

– Don't stop

– Don't edit (1013)

In other words do not revise as you go along and once you have started writing keep going. If you make an error then leave it and if you can't think of a word or phrase then leave a space to fill in later. Remember that nothing comes out perfectly the first time so instead of perfection aim for a draft that contains everything you want to say. (1081)

Of course, this process will only work when you know what it is that you are trying to write - and that is why the plan is so important. However, it is interesting to note that you do not have to start at the beginning. Rather, it suggests, it is far better to just get writing. So long as you cover everything by the end who cares about the order you write in.(1154)

However, the trainers of Writing Dynamics do suggest that you will need to add some colour into your text. Facts on their own can be pretty dry. So how can you develop your ideas? Some examples of what you can do to add life to your writing are: (1202)

1. Define or classify your subject e.g. 'The G90 is a new generation hybrid which, like the latest cars, can switch between petrol and battery power and will appeal to those people who are looking to cut down on CO_2 emissions.' (1244)

2. Compare and contrast e.g. unlike the conclusion made in the McGovern report our research has found that customers are definitely willing to buy at a higher price if the product can be delivered to their door. (1281)

3. Add testimonials e.g. To add weight to the vital issue of online demand here is a quote by John Davies, the CEO of UK Demand who said: "If we don't adopt the right web strategy, we will struggle to compete at Christmas and won't meet market expectations." (1328)

And there are other ways of adding colour too, such as backing up what you are saying with examples, outlining the consequences of your argument or describing the benefits of your case. (1360)

The Edit factor

Once you have drafted your piece Writing Dynamics then leads you to the most important step of all - editing. (1383)

For participants on the courses, this invariably means cutting down on what they have written, not adding to it. In trying to ensure they get their message across most people write too much and the impact of this is that the person reading gets bored or confused. (1431)

Editors know this and that is why they are so ruthless with their red pens! Here are three areas to which 'would be' writers should pay particular editing attention. (1459)

i. Are you managing your reader's attention? If your sentences are too long or complex then break them down. Shorter sentences will help you to be clear and concise and make it easier for readers to follow what you are saying. Additionally, add variety. If the first sentence in every paragraph you have written starts with the same word e.g. 'I ' or 'The' then your readers' attention will start to waver. Vary the length of your paragraphs and vary the words you start with. (1544)

ii. Create movement with more active writing. Most passive sentences contain some form of the verb 'to be'. So if you want to develop a more active style of writing, then look out for these words ... am, is, was, were, be, being, been. Once you have spotted that you are using the passive voice then change it. Put the 'doer' before the verb and the 'doee' after the verb. So 'The director wrote the report' is active while 'The report was written by the director' is passive. (1632)

iii. Create more energy by finding the action. Replacing long nouns with verbs will enliven your writing still further. Here is an example. 'We would appreciate your signature on the contract'. This is terribly slow compared to 'Please sign the contract.' Similarly 'We'd like your clarification of the matter' can be replaced by the faster 'Please clarify the matter.' So your challenge is to spot problem nouns and be more direct. (1703)

At The City of Edinburgh Council, training like Writing Dynamics, which delivers powerful techniques, that people can apply, is pure gold. The Council aims to be one of the best in the country and in order to meet its targets it needs to be in constant communication with its community about all the services it provides. In this respect Council managers who write hundreds of reports on everything from education and the environment to social work and transport need to be excellent communicators. Writing well isn't just a part of their job – it is a critical competency. (1798)

Said Pat Angus: "I went through the training myself and got something from every part of it. It was only when I started to pay close attention that I recognised how much 'Council speak' I was using and I suspect that is the same for all of us. So I started to work on having a clearer writing style, I now take more time planning how to get my message across and I've learned to cut out some of the padding I was using." (1882)

Other managers have been impressed with the course too. The anecdotal evidence suggests that it has taught people a process which eliminates the mystery around effective writing by giving them a clear system to follow. More than that, managers are finding that they are able to transfer what they have learned to their report writing without feeling restricted. Indeed, the feedback suggests that a certain amount of structure gives managers more confidence in their writing approach. (1957)

The acid test, however, will come a few months down the line when all the Council managers have undertaken the training and their latest reports have filtered through the system. "I know that the managers who have taken this training believe that they have made a big improvement but will our Councillors and our community notice a significant difference?" asked Pat Angus. "I will be asking for feedback and I expect them to find that the writing is sharper and clearer." (2040)

So the final question is this. Do people in your business or organisation need to improve their writing? As a writer myself I was surprised that a two day course had such an impact – but the conclusion I came to is that it does. No bull. (2087)

PANEL 1 Golden Bull Award Winner

Australian Taxations Office for its Goods and Services legislation 'For the purpose of making a declaration under this Subdivision, the Commissioner may:

a) treat a particular event that actually happened as not having happened; and

b) treat a particular event that did not actually happen as having happened and, if appropriate, treat the event as:

i) having happened at a particular time; and

ii) having involved particular action by a particular entity; and

c) treat a particular event that actually happened as:

i) having happened at a time different from the time it actually happened; or

ii) having involved a particular action by a particular entity (whether or not the event actually involved any action by that entity).' (2210)

PANEL 2 More bull

The following pieces of writing have all been awarded the Golden Bull by The Campaign for Plain English over the past few years (2237)

Trilogy Telecom (for an e–mail to a customer)

'BT have started processing the first stage of our MPF orders i.e. the line test and production of a line characteristics report. However with the second stage (i.e. physically installing the metallic facility path between the customers line and the Trilogy equipment) they will only walk one or two orders through the system Thursday of next week.'

(N.B. "Physically installing the metallic facility path" is better known as "laying the cable"!) (2316)

Jungle.com (The company was asked 'Do you still sell blank CDs?' Instead of simply saying 'No', they replied)

'We are currently in the process of consolidating our product range to ensure that the products that we stock are indicative of our brand aspirations. As part of our range consolidation we have also decided to revisit our supplier list and employ a more intelligent system for stock acquisition. As a result of the above certain product lines are now unavailable through jungle.com, whilst potentially remaining available from more mainstream suppliers.' (2405)

Lloyds Pharmacy (Rather than simply admit an assistant had dispensed the wrong strength of tablet, and that this mistake had not been picked up by the pharmacist, they wrote this apology.)

'The cognitive process that staff will go through when interpreting prescriptions and selecting drugs is almost intuitive in that the prescription will be read, a decision is then made in the mind of the individual concerned and they will then make a selection based on what they have decided. When an error is made either mentally or in the physical selection process it is difficult for the individual concerned to detect their own error because in their own mind they have made the correct selection.' (2520)

Information on Writing Dynamics can be found on www.illumine.co.uk/writing-dynamics.htm

Forget the standard presentation ... what we want from those people whose role it is to stand up and speak to us is for them to be genuine, spontaneous and engaging. Here Clive Lewis looks beyond the basics of presentation to how leaders, managers and front line staff can learn to think on their feet. (55)

SILVER TONGUES & FAST FEET

Who wouldn't want to have that ability to say the right thing at the right time ... to speak off the cuff, to improvise, even to wing it? We admire greatly those people who have this ability to be spontaneous – and rightly so. If you want to become an engaging speaker, a dynamic leader or a silver-tongued sales executive then you need to master the ability to think on your feet. (133)

But what is this gift of the gab, and can anyone do it? One way of explaining this quality is to consider that it allows you to go 'off piste' but stay in control when speaking in front of an audience. And it's my contention that you don't have to have kissed the blarney stone before you are successful at it. (193)

But having defined it, is spontaneous speaking an important quality to develop? I believe it is. You only have to think back to the last presentation you had from someone who was reading from a pre-prepared script, or speaking only from a series of PowerPoint slides, to get a sense of how stilted communication can be when it is being driven by inflexible thinking. (259)

But would you dare to wing it when running your next meeting or giving your next public address? Most people wouldn't but it's my bet that you might completely change your mind if a) you felt confident about doing it and b) it gave you a much better chance of achieving the outcome that you wanted. In fact, if you felt confident of success it would be hard to argue against such an approach. (332)

Fear and excitement

However, before I explain how you can wing it, let me first just deal with any fears you might have about improvising. (357)

You don't have to look far to find some clear examples of people who try to be spontaneous only to fall flat on their faces. If you have ever seen the performance of those eager candidates in either Dragons' Den or The Apprentice, you will be quite aware of the process. Regularly caught off guard by what appear to be very reasonable questions, many of these would-be entrepreneurs simply fail to cope when asked to be authentic and say what they think. And as viewers we watch wide-eyed as these young hopefuls veer wildly off track, start providing far too much detail or simply lose their heads. Predictably they then get booted off the show. (474)

Now it may, of course, be mildly entertaining to see the howlers that people make when under pressure but what should they have done? The answer is this - they should have learned how to improvise whilst still knowing exactly where they were heading. Let me explain. (521)

Your ability to speak persuasively and spontaneously needs to be underpinned by a better understanding of how your brain works. The relevant information here is that there are two sides to your brain – the logical left side and the intuitive right side. As someone who wants to be able to improvise, all you need to do is to learn how to use both sides together, in harmony. You can compare this skill to that of being a pilot. What you need is a computerised flight path which will get you flying in the right direction. That's the left side of your brain. Meanwhile, at any time, you can override the computer, make mid-course corrections and even go and talk to the passengers. And that's the skill of the right hand side of your brain. Translate this into the area of communication and you have disciplined eloquence or even, perhaps, reliable excitement! (673)

Of course some people are concerned that any structure will limit their spontaneity. But this isn't true. The mind processes information extremely quickly and presenters, in giving themselves structure to improvise, are actually helping themselves and their listeners in two extremely important ways. Firstly, structure provides a clear focus for an audience. It imposes order on the mass of information that speakers or presenters have at their fingertips. Secondly, structure is liberating. Much like driving a car, when you know where you are going you can then make decisions about whether to listen to the radio, make conversation or engage in some creative thinking whilst knowing all the time that you are travelling on the right road. (790)

There is one other point to note here and that is to remember that the most powerful speakers are always less interested in what they are saying and more interested in what their listeners are receiving. Communication is the response you get – and anyone who is in the business of communicating, and who ignores this reality, will have a painfully hard path ahead of them. People who want to introduce spontaneity into their speaking must be especially aware of this. It may be exciting for you to talk from your expertise or your enthusiasm but in order to get your message across you will still need to be precise, unambiguous and clear. (902)

Pithy and punchy

So let me now talk about the way you need to plan for any talk or presentation that you are giving. The three 'must dos' are as follows:

1. Find the right theme for your audience

2. Structure your plan so that you can deliver on that theme persuasively

3. Adapt to listeners' reactions as you speak (960)

In the case of the main theme around which you are talking it is extremely helpful if you have a pithy and punchy headline which sums up your topic. This may sound obvious but even at this initial stage you should be engaging your creative right brain. What will add colour, imagination and excitement to your talk? Get creative and find a headline that stimulates your audience's curiosity so that they arrive in an inquisitive frame of mind. (1038)

As to how to structure your speaking, this is even more critical for anyone who wants to be able to improvise. The reality is that when it comes to thinking on your feet your plan will help your engagement by imposing order on your talk. And the three essential planks of your planning process are to define the central core of your topic, to separate out ideas so that they are distinct and to create momentum in your speaking so that you move your listeners smoothly from point A to B to C. (1130)

As to what precise structures to use when planning, here are three templates which have proven to be highly effective and which you can use for almost any talk or presentation you are giving. (1164)

1. The clock plan. This plan is one that divides your talk into chunks of time. If you are leading a project, for example, you might structure your talk into the following phases: i) where we are now; ii) the next six months; and iii) the situation in 12 months time. (1217)

2. The globe plan. This plan packages the key topics into chunks of space. So, for example, in this plan you might have as your main theme 'Doing business across the world'. It may then be broken down into: i) existing customers in the UK; ii) opportunities for expansion in mainland Europe; iii) untapped potential in South East Asia.(1276)

3. The triangle plan. This plan proposes that you are moving from one vantage point to another. So, for example, let us consider the

main theme to be 'The new IT system'. In this case the plan might look at the issues from the perspective of: i) what the end users need; ii) what customers will get out of it; iii) what the IT department can deliver. (1344)

These are three pretty straightforward plans which can help any speaker to marshal their ideas and there are many more. However, whatever structure you use, the point when it comes to improvisation is that it allows you to stay on track. Without structure any improvising can derail you and your audience. Billy Connolly might get away with wild digressions but only because he's extremely entertaining. For most of us we need our structure to support our spontaneity. Then we can start to have fun, using our intuitive brain to bring images, stories, sensation and imagination into play. (1441)

This way of combining structure and imagination is ideal for any presenter who wants to improve their ability to improvise. However here is a handy hint for first time users. Try numbering your sections as you go through your presentation so that you can remember where you are. This really is as simple as: i) the heading; ii), the main chunks - a, b and c and iii) the conclusion with its reminder of how it fits into the main theme. Numbering won't only keep you on track it will also help your audience to see exactly where you are heading and where you have got to. (1554)

Of course it is also worth remembering that not all improvisation happens when you are ready for it. Presenters may also want to be spontaneous when answering questions – see panel 2. Whatever the situation, however, just remember that thinking on your feet isn't about having every single possible fact at your fingertips. Rather it's about becoming more efficient by using your understanding of how the brain works to significantly improve your performance. Often it's about less rather than more. So don't try to cram everything into your sessions but rather keep your message simple and clear and use appropriate colour to make it memorable. (1662)

Relating gives you wings

The point to underline here is that structure is not enough. It will be a dead weight if it is all you rely on. You need to take managed risks. If you know your subject then you have to remember that you have all sorts of anecdotes, bits of research and associated ideas on which to call. More than that, what every audience really wants is interaction. So provoke them with your insights and give them a chance to ask you questions. Trust that your store of knowledge will be enough and build up an awareness that your audience wants you to do well and isn't anticipating your failure. More than this, nobody expects you to know everything – so be playful and engaging and turn your talk into more of a relationship than a lecture. Then, when the time is right, bring it back to the subject in hand and move on. (1818)

So remember, improvisation is only another way of saying that you need to be flexible. Your challenge, if you want to be engaging, is to find a way to be authentic and to use structure to support you. Your confidence in knowing where you are going will transmit to the people you are speaking to and the ability you have for interplay between you and your audience is critical. That is why managers and leaders want to learn the skill of thinking on their feet. It builds intimacy and trust and creates intellectual and emotional bridges between a speaker and his or her audience. This form of 'winging it' is truly skillful and, in comparison, reading from a speech, eyes glued to the text, is like flying blind. (1944)

PANEL 1: What can possibly go wrong?

When people decide to have a go at improvising in the middle of a presentation they are making, there are four traps that they need to be aware of. These are as follows:

1. The presenter goes off track. Take the example of a trainer asked a question about his subject. With too much information to impart he sets off into what he thinks is an interesting discussion

about a particular line of thinking. To him it may be a clear path but to the listener it can quickly seem as though it has little relevance to the main topic. (2051)

2. The speaker starts to go round and round. In this case the presenter may think they have to provide a new insight into the subject that they have just been talking about. So they go around again, making some points again and adding new ones just for good measure. The impact on the listener? They will quickly get exhausted trying to follow the trail of thought. (2118)

3. The presenter takes the fast and furious route. Some presenters, when they enter the unchartered territory of improvisation, feel that they have so much to say that they start to talk at breakneck speed. It's as though they feel they have to cram everything they know into a short period of time. The audience is stunned into silence but this is not because they understand the points being made. (2188)

4. Finally, the speaker becomes a data head. There are those speakers who, when asked questions, take it as an invitation to get into technical detail. This may be a defence or it may be real enthusiasm but too much detail is invariably of little use to the listener. (2237)

PANEL 2: Answer the question

The structures of 'Thinking on your feet' work very well for speakers who want or need to be able to answer questions in a direct and engaging way. Again the approach is about getting your audience from A (where they are), through B (the main points you want to make) and on to C (your conclusion). (2298)

Questions are not an invitation for you to show off your knowledge but, rather, to re-emphasise the clarity of your presentation. In this respect you are not transmitting but helping people to receive. So all you have to do is think of your core theme and make sure you are answering the question in a language that the listeners can understand. (2371)

And here's a trick worth knowing. Fewer, not more, words will help your audience. So be aware that every audience can spot padding and that it will not persuade or engage them. What you want instead is a leaner, punchier, more convincing style. (2448)

The approach to effective oral communication covered in this article is called Think on your feet. Details can be found at www.illumine.co.uk/course-communication-skills.htm

Facilitation isn't only a skill that can help teams to see where they are being blocked; it can also make a specific difference to team decision making. Anthony Landale reports on a new facilitation approach.

MUST HAVE CONSENSUS

Collective intelligence has been called the process of enhancing the group IQ and, as such, it is an extremely attractive proposition for managers and leaders. But how exactly do you get to mine this intelligence? In principle we all know that we can achieve more when we work together with others – but in practice how can we make it happen? (99)

The answer to this conundrum lies in facilitation – and, more specifically, in the way that facilitators can help people to reach consensus. Let me explain.

Facilitation has become necessary in today's business world because it is understood that the process of how something gets done can often get in the way of the task itself. Looked at in another way, while the individuals within a group or team may be extremely talented and motivated this doesn't mean that they know how to work together effectively. (185)

Facilitators are trained to work with this dynamic – ensuring that issues such as relationships, beliefs and values are included as an essential part of the team's ability to perform. (215)

As a simple example of the need for such facilitation we only need to look at the scenario of a conflict within a team. We've all surely been in situations where simmering resentment or frustration has undermined the efforts of a team – but how many managers know how to address such issues constructively? And if they don't address it then what happens? Conflicts don't just go away.

Indeed when they are left unresolved tensions often fester and impact negatively on people and projects. The facilitator who is aware of these dynamics can bring them to the surface and resolve them. (315)

When it all goes wrong

Many people will, of course, already have some experience of facilitation. Remember when you helped people who didn't know each other to find common ground. Remember when you tried to settle an argument, fairly. Remember when you ran a meeting. That's the territory we are talking about. However, while some people are naturally brilliant at facilitating, most are not. (383)

I have a colleague who thought she had landed a plum job when a company asked her to mix business and pleasure on the ski slopes of Austria. It sounded so easy – facilitate a series of team meetings in the morning, ski with the team in the afternoon. All expenses paid for a week. What could be better? (438)

It wasn't quite the breeze she imagined. "I thought facilitation was just flying by the seat of your pants," she told me later. "But before I knew it the team were at each others' throats." (473)

What had actually occurred was this. At the first meeting, on the first morning, people in the team started telling each other what they really thought about one another. They weren't complimentary and my friend had no idea what to do. When it was clear that she couldn't recover the situation it got worse. She got the blame, publicly, for letting the whole thing get out of hand. The team disintegrated, the trip was a disaster and she had learned a salutary lesson. (556)

Now this may have been an unusual set of circumstances but it highlights the danger of thinking that facilitation is easy. Often it isn't. So what exactly is facilitation all about and what exactly do you do as a facilitator? (596)

Facilitation depends on the context. There is no set script. You have to be able to respond to whatever is going on with the people you are working with. However, if you are a manager and you want to get the best out of your team so that everyone is contributing then you will need to develop the following range of essential skills: (659)

1. You will need to develop generous listening skills. This means listening for everything that is said and not said; listening for intent, for commitment, for purpose.

2. You will need to learn how to speak powerfully, timing your remarks so that they encourage, support, challenge or inspire people in your team.

3. You will need to know how to ask penetrative questions that open up discussions or shine a light on issues where people are stuck.

4. You will need to be able to challenge people either directly or through feedback. And you will need to be able to do so compassionately.

5. You will need to be able to value people so that they feel acknowledged and feel encouraged to speak out

6. You will need to be a great observer, watching everything that is happening and bringing what is important to the attention of the group

7. You will need to be able to contain people. This means that you won't mind if people get angry or upset, it means you will be able to keep the boundaries and you won't take what happens too personally. (848)

RapidConsensus

So by using such skills as these you can facilitate teams and groups to deal with the invisible factors that often bedevil projects. But facilitation can be much more specific that this and recently a new approach for facilitators has been developed that focuses on how to get people to collaborate and reach consensus fast. And according to the company behind it, illumine Training, the process is quite straightforward. (919)

Clive Lewis is illumine's Managing Director and he explained: "We all know in business that decision-making can be a problem. Sometimes it is very slow and sometimes the decisions made don't make much sense to those who are asked to carry them out. This is very frustrating for everyone concerned. What we recognised at illumine was that an approach was needed to help people in teams make good decisions, own those decisions and take action based on those decisions that helped accelerate projects. (1002)

"RapidConsensus was developed with exactly this in mind. It is a facilitative approach which helps people to understand exactly where they are now and where they want to be. Following that, it gets the whole team to consider what their options are and to identify what actions they need to take to get there." (1056)

Now while this sounds like a straightforward enough model, according to Lewis it's a revelation when people actually work through each of the stages together. "RapidConsensus is an elegant process which helps people in a team come together and view the issue at hand by winding back to the beginning. People who want to hurry through the decision-making process and get straight into action miss the whole point – namely, that for good decision-making you need to engage the whole group and mine their collective intelligence. And actually the approach doesn't take long. But it does require a range of facilitation skills including having exceptional listening , building the environment where people engage freely in dialogue and knowing how to work with group dynamics." (1181)

The principles explained

So how exactly does this approach make such an impact?

First of all, the RapidConsensus approach is based on the principle that people own what they help to create. In other words, people need to feel engaged and enthusiastic about an outcome before they commit to it. Just telling people to act in a certain way, or imposing a decision, will inevitably fail to engage people's energy or motivation. (1253)

Unfortunately many managers and leaders either like to tell people what to do or fear that a group process will lead to poor decisions being made. But this isn't so. The best decisions are made when everyone is asked for their input – and managers need to recognise that it is only when they allow space for people to contribute their thinking that commitment and ownership will occur. (1321)

In addition to this, it is clear to most people who work in teams that the brightest and most articulate people do not always have all the answers. In fact a room left to its own devices will tend to work on less than 50% of the information and knowledge available in the room. You have surely seen this happen when the most dominant person by status or personality will control the conversation while the more reserved people will contribute little or nothing. (1404)

So what can be done about this? One method used in RapidConsensus that addresses this problem directly is for the facilitator to have the same question addressed concurrently by separate groups. Then, when these sub-groups report on the issue it is certain that everyone has had the opportunity to contribute. Furthermore, if each group has reached the same conclusion the facilitator knows that the decision made will have everyone's support. (1478)

Distinct from this – and another key aspect of this consensus based approach – occurs when the facilitator helps the group or team to identify the future that they want to create. (1510)

What this means in practice is getting people to articulate as powerfully as possible where they want to be. This is important because there are many more creative possibilities in the future than there are in the present. To paraphrase Einstein: 'You cannot solve problems with the same level of thinking that got you here.' (1565)

In this process of breakthrough thinking it is the facilitator's role to listen to everything and defend nothing. This requires them to remain neutral and feedback what everyone has said accurately to the whole group. People come into the room from many different viewing platforms, for example production, marketing, sales, maintenance, administration ... all see the world and the problems within it through their own lens. However it is the culmination of all these perspectives and interdependencies which provides a whole view of the situation. (1650)

As Clive Lewis explains: "Providing a process that allows everyone's views to be heard is a fundamental part of the RapidConsensus process. This allows the group to work on the best information and knowledge available to them.

In order to do this the facilitator has to operate as an open conduit. This means they are 100% present and able to remain open to all the input from the group. Things will be said that the facilitator may or may not agree with, yet to maintain the open dialogue, they must not defend a view but treat all views with equal respect and space." (1753)

Speed and quality

Lewis also suggests that the speed of the process contributes directly to the quality of group decisions. "People have different speeds of thinking and interacting yet we all have a rapid cognition capability that works best under time pressure. The first intuitive response is, often, better than a long thinking process. As the room becomes a safe place to explore ideas the ability of the room to process complex information and make decisions also speeds up. (1837)

"With speed the group will also start to experience lateral leaps in their thinking which characterises the creative process. Well facilitated groups surprise themselves with the speed with which they can process information and make decisions. And experience has shown us that the quality of these decisions is high as continued progress and breakthroughs are made after the workshop." (1897)

In essence, the promise of RapidConsensus is that it addresses that intractable issue – namely how to make good, fast decisions which the whole team own. And it does this by getting everyone to start together and talk together in the same room. As economic guru John Kay said: "Despite the internationalisation of markets, despite air travel, despite technology there are still things done best by people who find themselves in the same room". Lewis agrees. "The best dialogue comes when people stop hiding behind their roles and start talking on the same level. And in this respect this process is based around the fundamentals of human interaction. Once people stop and listen to one another and take in different viewpoints, it becomes apparent that wisdom can be found everywhere. (2049)

"I think all people want to work in collaborative and creative environments where they feel heard and valued. The RapidConsensus approach gives people an experience that they want to make the norm for their professional and personal lives." (2087)

Further information on RapidConsensus can be found at
www.illumine.co.uk/course-rapid-consensus.htm

Make your own notes here

Make your own notes here

MORE ABOUT THE AUTHORS

CLIVE LEWIS

Clive Lewis is, above all else, a speed-reading practitioner. He was first introduced to speed-reading and related techniques in 1978 and used them successfully when studying for his business studies degree, in qualifying as a management accountant and in his practice as a 'Big 6' management consultant.

In 1996 Clive decided to set up illumine, a training consultancy dedicated to teaching speed-reading, mind mapping and memory techniques and the company is now a leader in the field having trained several thousand people in the UK, Europe, India, North America and the Middle East.

Clive is fired by the belief that anyone can learn to speed-read and consign to the past the threat of information overload. His training, and this book, bring together the related elements of technique, attitude and belief as they relate to the INSEAK reading strategy. He can be contacted on +44 (0)1753 866633 or on clive@illumine.co.uk

ANTHONY LANDALE

Anthony Landale is an experienced business writer and an executive coach. He is the editor of The Gower Handbook of Training & Development and the co-author of The Fast Facilitator. He has also been the editor of Management Skills & Development magazine and People Performance. He can be contacted on +44 (0)1608 811861 or on anthonylandale@aol.com

WHERE TO GO NEXT

If you would like to further your speed-reading skills by working with Clive Lewis and his team you can contact Illumine on -+44 (0)1753 866633 or visit www.illumine.co.uk. Illumine runs half day and full day speed-reading and accelerated information management courses for businesses across the UK and internationally. Clive is also available for conference speaking and keynote presentations. He also offers 1:1 coaching.

FURTHER READING

Butler G & Hope T, Manage your Mind, OUP (1997)

Buzan T & Buzan B, The Mind Map Book, BBC Books (1995)

Covey S, The Seven Habits of Highly Effective People, Simon & Schuster (1994)

Dilts R, From Coach to Awakener, Meta Publications (2003)

McDermott I & O'Connor J, NLP & health, Thorsons (2001)

O'Connor J & McDermott I, Way of NLP Thorsons (2001)

Dryden G and Vos J, The Learning Revolution, Aylesbury: Accelerated Learning Systems Ltd (1994)

Goleman D, Emotional Intelligence, Bloomsbury, (1996)

Landale A, Gower Handbook of Training & Development, Gower (1999)

Ratey J, A user's guide to the brain, Abacus (2001)

Ramachandran V.S, Phantoms in the Brain, Harper Collins (1999)

Restak R, Mozart's Brain and the Fighter Pilot, Crown Publications (2002)

Sherwood D, Unblock your Mind, Gower (1998)